Dark Goddesses

Unveil Secret Power
of Lilith, Morrigan, Hekate and more,

With rituals, exercises, meditations
to Unlock Your inner Goddess

TEMPLUM DİANAE

- MEDİA -

claim included content

Congratulations on getting this book!
If you want to attract and manifest more Love and Abundance and Find Out about spirituality and topics, then join Templum Dianae's community and get guided meditation MP3 for awakening your inner self.

This guided meditation is designed to manifest your inner dream in your daily life.

templumdianae.com/en/bookmp3/

IF YOU DON'T KNOW TEMPLUM DIANAE YET

Wayfarer, if you've picked up this book, it's not by accident. You've been called. Let me make this very clear: what you are about to dive into is not a fluffy exploration of divine femininity, all pastel pinks and roses. This is about real power. This is about *you* stepping into the dark, raw energy of the goddesses who have been feared, worshiped, and misunderstood for centuries. If you're here for comfort, you won't find it. But if you're here to unlock the part of yourself that has been buried beneath the layers of expectations, doubt, and fear… then keep reading.

This book will tear open the doors to your soul and show you the power of the Dark Goddesses—*Lilith, Hekate, Morrigan*, and many others. These goddesses don't coddle. They challenge, they provoke, and they force you to confront the parts of yourself that you've been running from. And let's be honest, haven't you run long enough? You're here because something in your life is missing. You want more than just survival. You want to thrive, to attract abundance, and to truly stand in your power.

Let me be blunt. Too many books promise transformation and deliver disappointment. That won't happen here. This is not for the faint-hearted or the half-committed. This book, *Dark Goddesses: Unveil the Secret Power of Lilith, Morrigan, Hekate, and More to Unlock Your Inner Goddess*, is your gateway to transformation—if you're ready to claim it.

Now, you might be wondering, *why should I trust this book?* What makes this different from all the other empty promises? The answer lies in the source. This book is brought to you by **Templum Dianae Media**, a project born out of the **Templum Dianae blog**, an authority in witchcraft, pagan practices, and spiritual awakening since 2013. Not just some random online platform, Templum Dianae is *written by witches, for witches.* It's a community, a movement, and a force that's been changing lives for over a decade.

Let's get into the facts. Over **247,000 people every month** come into contact with the material created by Templum Dianae across all channels. That's hundreds of thousands of people who are learning, growing, and transforming through our books, blogs, and teachings. And this isn't just theory—it's real-world results. We publish hundreds of books every year in **six languages**, spreading ancient wisdom and modern insights around the globe. We're reviving long-lost grimoires and releasing cutting-edge guides to help women like you rise into their full power.

Still skeptical? Let me share some testimonials from women who've connected with Templum Dianae and have seen massive transformations in their lives.

"Before I found Templum Dianae, I was stuck—spiritually, financially, and emotionally. But after immersing myself in their materials, everything shifted. Not only did I feel more connected to myself and my spirituality, but my business took off. I'm now making more money than I ever imagined." — Alessandra, Entrepreneur

"Templum Dianae helped me understand that I wasn't broken. I just needed to reconnect with my true power. Since following their rituals and guidance, I've manifested more abundance and found the love I had been longing for." — Helena, Healer

These are not isolated stories. Thousands of women, just like you, have found their lives transformed by the teachings and rituals of Templum Dianae. And now, it's your turn. But here's the thing: you need to be willing to *do the work*. This isn't about lighting a candle and hoping for the best. This is about diving deep into the darkness, confronting your shadows, and unleashing the goddess within.

The goddesses in this book—Lilith, Hekate, Morrigan, Medusa, Kali, and more—are not passive, nurturing figures. They are warriors, witches, and rulers of the unseen realms. They will push you to embrace the parts of yourself that society has told you to hide. They will demand that you honor your desires, your ambitions, and your deepest truths.

If you're ready to step into that power, keep reading. If you're ready to connect with the goddesses who embody independence, strength, transformation, and fierce feminine energy, then this is your path.

Let's be honest, Wayfarer—you didn't pick up this book because you're comfortable. You're here because something is *missing*. Maybe it's your confidence, your sense of purpose, your ability to attract what you want. Maybe it's a deeper connection to your own spirituality. Whatever it is, this book will help you find it. But only if you commit.

Templum Dianae has been delivering transformational teachings since its inception. With **hundreds of books published every year** and an ever-growing global community, we are the modern-day bridge to ancient wisdom. Our mission is simple: to empower witches, seekers, and spiritual warriors to embrace their full potential.

Now it's time for you to decide. Will you answer the call? Will you take the journey through the dark, to meet the goddesses who are waiting to guide you to your own power?

The choice is yours. But remember this: the Dark Goddess doesn't wait for permission. She is already within you, waiting for you to awaken her. This book is your invitation to that awakening. Don't close it. Don't turn away. Your transformation starts now.

İNDEX

Contents

THE İNNER GODDESS

Throughout the annals of human history, the enigmatic figures of the Dark Goddesses have stood at the crossroads of fear and reverence. Cloaked in mystery, their origins, roles, and true powers have both fascinated and unsettled civilizations across the globe. These powerful deities, often associated with the shadowy aspects of existence, represent the duality inherent in the human psyche—the balance between creation and destruction, light and darkness, fear and empowerment.

From the stormy shores of Celtic lands to the sun-scorched deserts of Egypt, every culture has woven tales of formidable goddesses who embody the profound forces of nature and the universe. In some pantheons, these Dark Goddesses were held in higher esteem than their benevolent counterparts, not merely out of fear but out of a deep respect for their undeniable influence over life and death. To invoke their names was to acknowledge the raw, unbridled power that shapes our world and our inner selves.

This book is an exploration—a journey into the archetypal realms of these Dark Goddesses. We will delve into what renders them so potent and significant, both in ancient times and for contemporary seekers of spiritual wisdom. By examining their myths, symbols, and the cultures that revered them, we aim to unveil the hidden aspects of the divine feminine that have been suppressed or misunderstood over the centuries.

Moreover, we will connect these ancient archetypes to modern psychological concepts, such as Carl Jung's theory of the shadow self. Just as Jung proposed that embracing our shadow is essential for personal growth, so too can engaging with the Dark Goddesses facilitate a deeper understanding of ourselves. By confronting and integrating these shadow aspects, we unlock the door to our own inner goddess—a source of profound strength, intuition, and transformation.

Our journey will take us through the rich tapestries of Greek, Egyptian, Mesopotamian, Slavic, Hindu, African, Celtic, and Norse mythologies. Unlike many studies that focus solely on the mythological narratives, this book seeks to provide a multilayered insight into their historical contexts and spiritual significance for modern practitioners. We will explore not only who these goddesses were but also how their influence persists today, offering guidance and empowerment to those willing to engage with their energies.

Whether you are new to spiritual practices or are seasoned in shadow work, goddess worship, neo-paganism, or other alternative paths, this book is designed to meet you where you are. It presents both theoretical and practical information in an accessible, beginner-friendly manner, ensuring that all readers can relate to and enrich their spiritual journeys. If you are curious about diverse spiritual traditions or wish to deepen your understanding of dark deities from a specific culture, consider this book your companion on a path of discovery and personal evolution.

In a world that often celebrates only the light, acknowledging the dark can be a radical and empowering act. If you resonate with the divine feminine and seek knowledge and inspiration from powerful female deities, this guide will illuminate the way. Through a profound and esoteric exploration of the darker facets of these goddesses, you will learn to appreciate the complexity of their symbolism and myths. More importantly, you will discover the immense empowerment they can bestow upon you when you embrace their teachings.

As we embark on this journey together, prepare to expand your spiritual wisdom and deepen your connection to the feminine divine. By understanding and embracing these powerful energies, you will unlock new dimensions of yourself and the world around you. The path may be challenging, but the rewards are transformative.

Are you ready to unveil the secret powers of Lilith, Morrigan, Hekate, and more? Are you prepared to unlock your inner goddess and step into a realm of profound self-discovery and empowerment?

If so, turn the page and let the journey begin.

access to feminine power

In a world that often dictates who women should be and how they should act, many find themselves disconnected from their true essence — their inner goddess. This disconnection can manifest as a feeling of powerlessness, a sense that one's life is being directed by external forces rather than inner desires and strengths. The journey to reclaiming this lost power begins with inner exploration, a courageous dive into the depths of the self to unearth the divine feminine that resides within.

Societal expectations have long imposed restrictive roles on women, emphasizing qualities like submissiveness, gentleness, and selflessness while discouraging expressions of strength, assertiveness, and autonomy. These cultural norms can lead women to suppress parts of themselves that don't align with these expectations, including their innate power and potential. This suppression creates an internal imbalance, leaving a reservoir of untapped energy and capabilities lying dormant.

Many women may feel an inexplicable void or restlessness, sensing that something vital is missing from their lives. This feeling often stems from the unacknowledged aspects of the self — the inner goddess waiting to be recognized and embraced. Without this acknowledgment, women may struggle with self-doubt, lack of direction, or a perpetual quest for external validation.

Accessing feminine power requires a deliberate and mindful journey inward. This process is about peeling back the layers of conditioning to reveal the authentic self beneath. It involves:

- **Self-Reflection**: Taking time to examine one's beliefs, values, and desires. Asking questions like "What do I truly want?" and "Who am I beneath the roles I've been assigned?" can begin this process.

- **Embracing Shadow Work**: Confronting and integrating the parts of oneself that have been suppressed or deemed unacceptable. This is where the Dark Goddesses become invaluable guides, as they embody the aspects of femininity that are often marginalized—such as anger, sexuality, independence, and transformation.

- **Cultivating Self-Love and Acceptance**: Learning to accept oneself wholly, including flaws and imperfections. This unconditional self-acceptance is a powerful act that nurtures inner strength and resilience.

- **Connecting with the Divine Feminine**: Engaging with the archetypes of the Dark Goddesses can facilitate a deeper connection with the divine feminine. Through rituals, meditations, and study, one can invoke their energies and wisdom.

As women delve into their inner worlds, they begin to dismantle the barriers that have kept their power at bay. This liberation leads to:

- **Self-Affirmation**: Affirming one's worth and capabilities without the need for external approval. This self-assurance is grounded in an authentic understanding of oneself.

- **Empowerment**: Recognizing and harnessing one's inherent strengths and abilities. Empowerment is not just about personal gain but also about influencing positive change in one's environment.

- **Accessing Hidden Potentials**: Discovering talents, passions, and facets of oneself that were previously unexplored. This can lead to new paths in personal development, career, relationships, and spirituality.

- **Living Authentically**: Aligning one's life with true values and desires, leading to greater fulfillment and joy.

The Dark Goddesses serve as powerful archetypes and allies in this journey. They represent the transformative forces of the feminine psyche — forces that are necessary for growth and renewal.

By studying their stories and integrating their lessons, women can draw upon these goddesses' strengths to navigate their own lives with confidence and purpose.

Accessing feminine power is not a destination but a continuous journey of self-discovery and growth. It requires patience, compassion, and a willingness to face both the light and dark within. As women embrace their inner goddesses, they contribute to a collective awakening of the divine feminine, fostering a more balanced and harmonious world.

This journey is deeply personal yet universally significant. Each woman's empowerment inspires others, creating ripples of change that extend beyond the individual. By unlocking their inner secret potentials, women not only transform their own lives but also pave the way for future generations to live authentically and powerfully.

Reflection Questions:

1. What aspects of yourself have you suppressed due to societal expectations?

2. How can you begin to explore and embrace your inner goddess?

3. In what ways can the archetypes of the Dark Goddesses inspire and empower you?

As you ponder these questions, remember that the path to accessing your feminine power is a sacred journey. It is an invitation to return home to yourself, to stand in your truth, and to live a life that honors the divine essence within.

UNDERSTANDING ARCHETYPE OF DARK GODDESS

As a seeker, you feel the pull to step into the darkness, to explore what lies beyond the familiar. This chapter is your guide into that realm, helping you understand the origins, symbolism, and profound meaning of the term **"Dark Goddess."**

We will journey through the multifaceted contexts of spirituality, psychology, and mythology across a rich tapestry of cultures and spiritual traditions. **By embracing the transformation that comes through darkness and shadow**, you will gain deeper insights and esoteric knowledge about the Dark Goddess archetype.

The **concept of the Dark Goddess** is not confined to a single culture or belief system. She is an archetype—a universal symbol—representing similar roles, attributes, and functions in different societies. **She dwells within the causal part of the spirit, known as the psyche**, a living presence that emerges from our deepest thoughts and magical intentions. **When you believe in her, she comes alive within you**, influencing your life in subtle yet profound ways.

Think of the Dark Goddess as a seed planted in the fertile soil of your mind. **Through your thoughts and beliefs, she grows and blossoms**, becoming a powerful force that guides and transforms you. *It's like nurturing a hidden garden within yourself, one that flourishes as you tend to it with awareness and intention.*

As New Age, pagan, and alternative spiritual paths have gained popularity, **the allure of these powerful dark beings has grown stronger. Why is that, you might wonder?** Because the Dark Goddess embodies **authenticity and diversity** — qualities that modern society often suppresses. **By embracing her, you shine a light on aspects of yourself and the world that have been overshadowed.**

Consider the parts of yourself that you have been told to hide or ignore. *Perhaps it's a passion that doesn't fit societal norms, or emotions that are deemed unacceptable.* **These repressed elements linger in the shadows**, much like the dark deities in ancient legends. **The Dark Goddess invites you to bring them into the light**, to heal and transform. **She guides you toward a rebirth**, freeing you from expectations and burdens that hinder your true self.

Her energy is potent. **She is a powerhouse**, capable of rewriting the story of your life. **By connecting with her, you unlock the divine feminine's freedom and empowerment**, reshaping your narrative in profound ways.

The **Dark Goddess** is but one facet of the divine feminine. Many seekers are drawn to goddesses who embody light and positivity. **But life isn't always sunshine and serenity**, is it? **Sometimes, you're compelled to delve into the goddess's shadow side**, for it is there that answers to your deepest pains and challenges reside.

Imagine facing a difficult period in your life — a loss, a betrayal, a profound disappointment. *In those moments, the comforting embrace of light may not be enough.* **It's in the depths of shadow that you find resilience**, the strength to confront and overcome adversity. **The Dark Goddess stands beside you**, a steadfast ally who understands the complexity of your emotions.

It's important to recognize that these deities are labeled "dark" not because they are malevolent, but because certain cultures misunderstood or feared them. In patriarchal societies, **powerful female deities were often associated with war and destruction**, their strength misconstrued as a threat. **Patriarchs claimed they harbored an unusual desire to spill blood**, casting them in a negative light.

But in cultures that honor dark feminine energies, **the Dark Goddess is embraced as an integral part of the whole**. She represents the necessary, though sometimes frightening, experiences of life. **While her lighter aspects nurture and heal, her darker sides teach you to fight, to confront your enemies — both external and within — and to overcome formidable obstacles**.

Imagine standing firm in the face of adversity, drawing strength from a source deep within. *It's like tapping into an ancient well of courage and resilience that empowers you to overcome any challenge.* **This is the gift of the Dark Goddess**.

In many legends and stories, **the Dark Goddesses were summoned to chase away true evil and purify what was tainted. They are warriors and protectors**, not destroyers. **By embracing their energy**, you learn not only to face the darkness but to transform it, emerging stronger and more authentic.

Jung and the Shadow Self

The Dark Goddess archetype is mysterious, destructive, chaotic, and often associated with the occult. Yet, it is also transformational, offering a holistic insight into oneself and nature. The nature of these female deities is dark, reflecting the experience of female empowerment. This nature perfectly embodies what the renowned psychologist Carl Jung called the **"shadow self."**

In many religions, the Dark Goddess represents the part of nature that should be avoided or prevented from flourishing. Despite differences in their stories, Dark Goddesses in Eastern and Western cultures were viewed similarly. In Western societies, the archetype was seen as a projection of patriarchy, associated with hostile intentions and warfare.

When it comes to human nature, darkness was something people were encouraged to stay away from. While it might seem wise to discourage embracing one's darkest self, **suppressing your shadow self prevents you from understanding your true nature, values, and spiritual needs.** As a searcher, you might feel the pull to explore this deeper part of yourself.

Delving into Jung's psychodynamics and theoretical analysis of the human psyche becomes essential here. Carl Jung was primarily concerned with the human psyche, but he and his students also researched the concept of the goddess, bridging psychoanalysis and esoteric practices. Jung referred to the goddess as **anima** or **anima mundi** — which means **world soul** — implying that we live in a goddess-centered world and that the goddess lives within each of us.

According to Jung, the Dark Goddess archetype is the manifestation of the **"shadow self,"** standing in opposition to the "**ego self.**" The self represents the entirety of the psyche, combining the subconscious and conscious parts. As the most authentic core of your being, the self gives rise to traits and characters, including the persona and the anima/animus—the gendered parts of the collective subconscious. The **anima** is how the male psyche envisions the feminine, and the **animus** is how the female psyche infers the male one. The persona is the part of yourself you present to the world.

Jung saw the ego as the core and main driver of your persona— the part you are conscious of and control through your actions. However, he believed there must be a balance to the ego. While treating patients, he discovered that deep down, people are always aware of their true nature and personality, even if they don't show this awareness to the outside world. He called this hidden part "**the shadow**" and argued that reaching it requires immense effort.

By raising awareness of your shadow self, you can identify the darkest aspects of your personality and acknowledge them as real parts of your existence. For most people, this goes against their every core belief, so they naturally resist conceding to their shadow self. The main reason for resistance can be found in the patriarchal theological concept of evil, which dictates that the dark part of oneself is bad and, therefore, must be repressed.

Jung called the process of raising self-awareness of one's complex nature **Individuation**. Facing your shadow is the first step on this journey. Instead of viewing the dark side as something to be ashamed of, Jung encouraged people to confront the part of themselves that prompts them to do negative things. He claimed that since these are natural parts of everyone's personality, **it's better to get to know them closely rather than avoid them as if they would lead to corruption.**

Jung's theory about the Dark Goddess archetype being the epitome of the shadow self offers a fantastic way to describe and experience internalized feelings. What's ineffable to some people, followers of Dark Goddesses can embrace as a natural experience without biases, doubt, or questions. **Regardless of your beliefs, the goddess teaches you about the importance of experience**, effectively validating the things you can't explain through rational thoughts and concepts.

Jung's theories provide an empowering and genuine intrinsic source of power in the Dark Goddess. Whether identifying her as an individual female divinity in a vast pantheon of deities or seeing her as the face of a multi-faceted goddess, this is exactly how the archetype is portrayed in several religions.

Supporting Jung's claims about the effort required to face the darkness within, many tales describe the high price paid by those approaching the goddess. **Known to bring people to the edge of extreme psychological exhaustion, these dark female forces demand a great deal.** You cannot simply hope for the best when encountering these deities. **Interaction with them is ill-advised unless you are truly prepared to handle their power.**

Practitioners often describe experiencing a significant negative shift when calling on a Dark Goddess. Considering Jung's theories, this is to be expected. **Confronting your dark self brings up many negative emotions, including fear, helplessness, anxiety, and weakness.** Yet, without experiencing these, you cannot learn your own strength. If you never face anything that upsets or scares you, how do you know you'll have the courage to overcome it? **Only by confronting your weaknesses can you understand what it takes to summon your strength.** *It's a powerful but much-needed lesson the archetype teaches.*

The goddesses also show that just as everyone can be compassionate and loving when empowered, **their power can also come from anger, pain, and other negative emotions and experiences — and use it for great purposes**.

Facing your dark self often results in the destruction of previous beliefs, but this is necessary to rebuild yourself. Before working with the Dark Goddess, you might be living driven only by the conscious part of yourself. Afterward, **you become whole and find your individual strength. This is where the true power of the Dark Goddess archetype lies.**

Over time, Jung's theories that tied the archetype to a person's personality and psyche became widely accepted. Some were purely intrigued by this mysterious power, while others realized the importance of further exploration of this highly neglected archetype. Interestingly enough, Jung viewed the Dark Goddess both as a female shadow self (**anima**) and the dark aspect of the male shadow (**animus**). This explains why so many people don't want to concede to this aspect within their psyche. **It goes against the male ego, which doesn't like to think it has weaknesses, fears, and insecurities.**

However, **the shadow knows these weaknesses exist**, and contrary to other popular beliefs, it's not evil or negative. The female shadow empowers the person to acknowledge this part of their psyche — weaknesses, faults, and all.

The multitude of Dark Goddesses you can work with have their own particular powers. **By summoning the ones you identify with or truly need, you can find the way forward in your empowerment journey.** For example, calling on a goddess symbolizing freedom and lust can help you suppress guilt about not following societal expectations blindly — *virtually no one does because it's impossible given how many there are and how baffling they can be*. Likewise, summoning a goddess of transformation can help you heal from past traumas and use them to illustrate growth.

Those following in Jung's footsteps helped transform the goddess from a simple archetype into a full-blown movement. They brought the archetype alive from the causal psyche and into the real world, proving its existence. This helped popularize the concept of the divine feminine, both in its own transcendent nature — which helps identify it in oneself — and as the driving force behind new and re-emerging religions that worship Dark Goddesses as transcendent divine beings.

Archetype Representations

In many cultures, **the Dark Goddess is seen as a sinister figure**, a female entity with origins rooted in ancient traditions far older than the myths of their benevolent counterparts. **She is known by many names — Mother of Blood, Mistress of Destruction —** titles that evoke both fear and awe. Popular religions and traditions often depict these dark deities as strikingly beautiful women in their prime, adorned in provocative attire or sometimes depicted in the nude. **Legends claim that in ancient times, these goddesses could only be appeased through human sacrifices**, and **their names were never to be spoken aloud**.

But **as a searcher**, you may sense there's more beneath these ominous portrayals. **These depictions, while shadowed in darkness, actually empower women beyond the nurturing goddess archetype**. Yes, their empowerment may come from associations with the occult and the mysterious, but **they play vital roles in personal evolution and collective growth**.

Female empowerment may be hidden behind esoteric concepts and misunderstood pagan practices, yet it's clear that by working on themselves and embracing their entire selves, **women can access this power. You don't have to conform to a serene and passive ideal to be powerful. The Dark Goddess isn't afraid to highlight the dark feminine principle. You don't have to adopt male behaviors to be as powerful as men. You can find empowerment within**, embracing your own nature to feel, behave, and grow as an equal. *Think of a lioness leading her pride with strength and grace.*

At the same time, **the archetype teaches men that acknowledging their weaknesses won't diminish their masculinity**. *Imagine a warrior who knows his vulnerabilities and* *turns them into strengths.* Followers of the Dark Goddesses learn that both genders have much more to offer than the qualities traditionally ascribed to them. **No one embodies a perfect ideal of never harming anyone or never making mistakes.** It's impossible. **If nothing else, you'll eventually hurt yourself.**

It's not uncommon for Dark Goddesses to be portrayed as opportunistic and vengeful, especially when punishing mortals. Yet, **true followers know that their wrath is never without cause. Sometimes, people need a powerful lesson to understand their connection to themselves and every being in the universe.** In their own way, **these goddesses teach empathy for everything and everyone around you, starting with yourself.** Whether you identify with a goddess of transformation or a warrior sorceress, **she will show you how to embrace your own values and character. The resonance you feel within is key to working with any archetype,** and **this is no different with the Dark Goddess.** *You might feel a stirring in your soul when you read about Hekate's wisdom or Morrigan's fierce protection.*

In some traditions, **the Dark Goddess is the unification of two opposing energies. You might believe, as Jung did, that a person is a whole made of two opposites within themselves.** By uniting the two divine powers, **a new, more powerful energy is born.** Unlike cultures that portray the archetype as undermining other forces, here, **the goddess is empathetic and noble, recognizing the need for balance in nature. Where there is light, there must be dark.** Therefore, opposing divine forces are both necessary and equal. **While portrayed as fearsome and relentless, Dark Goddesses display excellence of personal character — it's only a question of recognizing it. They are brave and courageous,** ready to confront any challenge in pursuit of victory.

Those exploring alchemy and similar practices believe that **embracing the Dark Goddess leads to radical transformation**, equipping a person to discover and cultivate empathy, love, and strength. While some of these qualities aren't typically associated with dark female energies, **many representations of the archetype show that evoking Dark Goddesses results in personal and spiritual growth. By learning empathy when working with a Dark Goddess, you become more capable of understanding your own shortcomings and others' as well**. After all, **who better to teach you about acceptance than someone considered terrifying, deadly, and unapproachable?** *It's like finding peace in the eye of the storm.* If you can accept them as they are, **you can embrace your own and other people's true personalities**, whether they are sensed as terrible, awesome, relatable, or anything else.

In most cultures, **the Dark Goddess represents something inexplicable, intangible, and uncontrollable. This is why working with them benefits every spiritual seeker**, even advanced practitioners. Often, what is ascribed to these qualities is considered bad or evil—including parts of yourself. **You have all these values within you, reminding you of your interconnectedness with everything in nature. Working with a Dark Goddess makes these aspects seem more real and tangible**. Many believe that archetypes can help deal with the unforeseen—**many of the Dark Goddesses' actions were seen as such in myths and beliefs**.

Those who previously feared the chaotic unknown within them learned, after working with a Dark Goddess, that just because there is something they didn't know about themselves, it doesn't mean they have to fear it. **This archetype of dark feminine power became an indispensable tool for self-development. Besides dissuading your fears from the hidden parts of**

yourself, the Dark Goddesses can show you how to integrate them into your conscious psyche.

The Dark Goddess symbolizes a profound yet challenging side of existence, forces that have shaped lives since the beginning of time. While interpretations and symbolism of these divine female energies vary across beliefs, **these infinite variations are why people with individual needs can identify with them. You can find your own way to work with one or more Dark Goddesses and embark on an eventful journey of discovery.**

GREEK ROMAN GODDESSES

While names like **Hera**, the majestic queen of the gods, and **Athena**, the wise and strategic goddess of wisdom and warfare, roll off people's tongues effortlessly, **there are other intriguing, less recognized figures in Greek mythology. As a searcher**, you might feel drawn to these enigmatic deities — **Persephone**, **Nyx**, and **Hekate** among them. Often labeled as 'dark' or 'evil', **understanding their origins and stories can shed light on their true natures**.

Consider **Persephone**. Her tale isn't one of malevolence but of profound transformation. **Whisked away to the underworld by Hades**, she becomes the queen of a realm often feared. Yet, **her journey symbolizes the cycle of nature**, where life undergoes periods of dormancy and renewal. **In spring, when Persephone returns to the Earth's surface, she brings with her the blossoms and beauty of the season**. *Think of the times you've emerged from a challenging period, feeling renewed and ready to bloom.* **She isn't evil; she embodies nature's perpetual cycle**.

Then there's **Nyx**, the primordial goddess of the night. **Older than the Olympian gods and goddesses**, she is the mother of essential concepts like Sleep and Death. **Nyx isn't evil**; she **embodies the tranquility and rest that the night provides**. **Her dark embrace is a time for recharging and renewal**, much like the peaceful moments you find under a starlit sky. *Imagine the serenity you feel during a quiet night, the world hushed, offering you space to reflect and restore.* **Nyx offers that sanctuary**.

Hekate, the goddess of crossroads, magic, and witchcraft, is another misunderstood figure. **In ancient Greece, people invoked her at crossroads to seek guidance and protection from unseen forces**. Her association with magic sometimes led to her being portrayed as sinister. However, **she is a symbol of the knowledge and power found in the unknown and the choices you make in life. Hekate stands at the thresholds,** illuminating the path ahead. *Picture yourself standing at a crossroads in life, uncertain which direction to take — Hekate lights the way, encouraging you to trust your intuition.*

These goddesses aren't truly evil or dark in the way you might think of villains. They represent different facets of life — change, the mysteries of the night, and the hidden wisdom within the world. **By exploring their stories, you gain a deeper appreciation for the complexities of life and nature. As a searcher,** you'll find that **delving into their tales reflects your own journey**, embracing both light and shadow.

With so much literature available today, **it's hard to separate the original stories from modern interpretations.** However, **learning how these goddesses were understood in their ancient context reveals their true significance and place. By unraveling the hidden truths and untold tales of Persephone, Nyx, Hekate, and their mysterious counterparts**, you shed light on the enigmatic and captivating aspects of Greek mythology that have long remained in the shadows.

Hekate

Hekate, goddess of crossroads, magic, and witchcraft, emerges from the shadows of ancient history with an aura of mystery and power. As a searcher delving into the depths of divine femininity, you encounter Hekate not just as a deity but as a guide through life's intricate pathways.

She is one of the Titans, primordial deities who existed before the Olympian gods and goddesses. Born to Perses and Asteria, Hekate embodies the triple goddess archetype—the maiden, the mother, and the crone—mirroring the moon's phases and the cycles of life. This connection weaves her essence into the very fabric of the universe's mysteries.

In the epic tales of old, Hekate's neutrality during the Titanomachy—the great battle between Titans and Olympians—sets her apart. She did not choose sides, and thus avoided the fate of imprisonment that befell many Titans. Her ability to navigate between light and dark, life and death, grants her a unique place among the gods. She moves through liminal spaces, those in-between realms where few dare to tread.

Hekate's association with crossroads is central to her mythology. In ancient Greece, travelers would leave offerings at crossroads, seeking her protection and guidance. These places symbolize life's choices and transitions. Standing at a crossroads yourself, you might feel her presence, an unseen force guiding you through uncertainty. She opens the gates between the mortal world and the spirit realm, offering wisdom when the path ahead seems unclear.

Magic and witchcraft are realms where Hekate reigns supreme. Under the cloak of night, followers would invoke her during rituals and spells, especially those tied to the moon. Her torches pierce the darkness, illuminating both the physical and metaphorical shadows. She guards the mysteries of the occult, and those who seek her favor believe she can grant profound knowledge and power. It's not simply about wielding magic; it's about understanding the unseen forces that shape our lives.

Consider the myth of Hekate and the abduction of Persephone. When Hades took Persephone to the underworld, her mother Demeter was consumed by grief. Hekate, bearing her torches, aided Demeter in the search for her daughter. Together, they navigated the darkness, symbolizing hope and guidance amidst despair. Hekate's role here is not of an evil force but of a compassionate helper, bridging the gap between the living and the dead.

In the tales of heroes, Hekate appears time and again. She aided the Greeks during the Trojan War, offering guidance and protection. Medea, the famed sorceress and priestess of Hekate, invoked the goddess's powers in her own magical practices. When Theseus ventured into the labyrinth to face the Minotaur, Hekate provided him with light and wisdom, ensuring his safe return. She is a facilitator of great deeds, supporting those who dare to seek her aid.

Dogs often accompany Hekate in mythological depictions. The howling of dogs at night was believed to signal her presence. They are sacred to her, symbols of loyalty and guardianship. In some stories, she can even transform into a dog, emphasizing her close bond with these animals. Their keen senses and protective nature reflect her own watchfulness over the thresholds between worlds.

Hekate's nightly walks are shrouded in intrigue. During the dark moon, she is said to roam the earth, accompanied by restless spirits and the haunting sounds of the night. Offerings left at crossroads during these times were meant to appease her and seek her blessings. It's a reminder of her dominion over the unseen, the aspects of existence that lie just beyond ordinary perception.

She also played a role in the quest for the Golden Fleece. Jason and the Argonauts sought her assistance to navigate treacherous waters and overcome daunting challenges. Hekate provided them with knowledge and guidance, showcasing her willingness to aid those on perilous journeys. Her wisdom is a beacon for heroes and seekers alike. In the myth of Perseus and Medusa, Hekate's influence is evident. She provided Perseus with a polished shield to use as a mirror, allowing him to face Medusa without succumbing to her petrifying gaze. This act underscores Hekate's role as a protector and a purveyor of clever solutions. She empowers others to confront fears and overcome obstacles.

Hekate's guardianship extends to the realm of childbirth. Mothers would invoke her to protect their newborns, trusting in her ability to ward off evil spirits. She watches over the vulnerable, ensuring safe passage into life. Her influence at these critical moments highlights her connection to both beginnings and endings.

Throughout these myths, Hekate is not portrayed as inherently evil or malevolent. Instead, she embodies duality—the balance between light and dark, life and death, known and unknown. Her realm encompasses the complexities of existence, the shadows that give depth to the light. She is a guide, a protector, and a source of profound wisdom.

As you explore Hekate's stories, you uncover layers of meaning that resonate with your own journey. She invites you to embrace the unknown, to find strength in the shadows, and to trust in the guidance that comes from within. Hekate's torches light the way not just for the heroes of old but for anyone willing to seek her wisdom.

Persephone

Persephone, daughter of Demeter — the goddess of agriculture — and Zeus, the king of the gods, was a radiant and joyful young goddess. **Her name, meaning "bringer of destruction" or "bringer of death," hinted at a destiny she could not yet fathom**. Everywhere she went, **she radiated life and growth**, a true symbol of the bountiful Earth.

Before her fateful encounter with Hades, Persephone lived a carefree life alongside her mother. She spent her days in sun-kissed meadows, nurturing flowers and crops. **Her laughter made flowers bloom; her joy caused fields to flourish**. The world thrived under her gentle touch.

Then came the day when the earth beneath her feet **cracked open without warning**. Hades, in his shadowy chariot, emerged and seized her. **Persephone's screams for help echoed into the silence**, unheard by those above. Taken against her will, she descended into the depths of the underworld. The bright, sunlit world she knew vanished, replaced by a shadowy realm of death.

In the underworld, **her despair was profound**. She longed for her mother, for the warmth of the sun, for the life she had lost. Yet, as time passed, **she began to assume her role as the queen of the dead**. She became a compassionate figure, offering solace to the souls who dwelled there. **Her strength and adaptability shone through**, embracing her new role despite the hardship.

As you delve into her story, **you might feel the weight of her transformation**. Above, the world mourned her absence. Demeter, grief-stricken, allowed the Earth to wither. **Crops failed; famine gripped the mortal realm**. The vibrancy Persephone once brought was nowhere to be found.

Demeter embarked on a relentless quest to find her beloved daughter. She searched every corner of the world, appealing to gods and mortals alike. Yet, **no one could reveal Persephone's whereabouts**; only Hades knew the truth.

Witnessing the suffering of both gods and mortals, Zeus decided to intervene. He urged Hades to release Persephone, recognizing that her return was essential to restoring balance. Hades agreed, but with one condition. **Because Persephone had consumed six pomegranate seeds in the underworld**, she was bound to spend six months of each year with him. **These months became the winter season**, when the world above lay shrouded in cold and darkness.

When Persephone returned to her mother, **their joyful reunion ushered in the spring**. The Earth burst into life once more. **Flowers bloomed where she stepped; fields turned green under her gaze**. The world celebrated the rebirth of nature and the return of its cherished goddess.

During her absence in the underworld, **the spirits there longed for her presence**. The realm of the dead felt emptier without her compassion and guidance. **Even in the land of shadows, she brought a light that was deeply missed**.

Persephone's story symbolizes the eternal cycle of the seasons. **Her descent into the underworld marks the arrival of winter**, a time of dormancy and reflection. **Her return heralds spring**, a time of renewal and growth. This cycle reflects her dual nature—**both the goddess of spring and the queen of the underworld**.

As a Dark Goddess, Persephone is associated with the mysteries of the underworld. **She is not evil**; her realm is one of shadows, death, and profound transformation. **Her journey from a carefree maiden to a powerful queen underscores her depth**

and resilience. Her story reminds us, as searchers of truth, of the delicate balance between life and death in the natural world.

Despite the darkness that surrounds her, **Persephone remains a compassionate and fair ruler**. She balances the scales of justice, providing comfort to souls in the afterlife. **Her annual return to the surface world brings joy and rejuvenation**, symbolizing the cycle of renewal that is essential to life.

In exploring Persephone's tale, **you uncover layers of meaning and wisdom**. She embodies both light and dark, growth and decay, joy and sorrow. **Her story invites you to embrace the complexities within yourself**, to find strength in adversity, and to recognize the cycles of change that shape your own journey.

Nyx

Nyx, a goddess as old as time itself, emerged from **Chaos**, the primeval void from which the entire cosmos came forth. **She embodies the night**, the very personification of darkness, and predates even the mighty Olympian gods. **A figure of profound beauty veiled in an aura of mystery**, her dominion extends far beyond the physical night. She governs the abstract concepts associated with darkness, making her a deity of immense influence. In the realm of night, she presides over sleep, dreams, and even death.

One of the most fascinating aspects of Nyx is her many and diverse offspring. Among her notable children is **Hypnos**, the god of sleep, known for bringing rest and dreams to mortals. **Thanatos**, the personification of death, represents the peaceful transition from life to the afterlife. **Moros**, the god of impending doom, underscores the inescapable fate that awaits all beings. **Eris**, the goddess of strife, thrives in the shadows, sowing discord and conflict often concealed under the cover of darkness. **Apate**, the deity of deceit, and **Geras**, representing the inevitable march of old age, are other offspring of Nyx. **This diversity of her children emphasizes the complexity of the forces she presides over**.

Nyx's presence in Greek mythology is all-pervasive, even though she does not feature as prominently as some other deities. She is often invoked during nighttime rituals when the world is shrouded in the mysteries of the dark. **Nyx holds immense power over transitions**, presiding over the shift from wakefulness to sleep, from life to death, and from consciousness to the ethereal world of dreams. Her influence extends into the depths of the subconscious, the realm of dreams, and the enigmatic forces that govern existence. **She is the true representation of a Dark Goddess.**

In the ancient city of Thespiae, Nyx was revered as the **Dark Virgin**, a guardian of mysteries and sacred rites. **Clad in her dark mantle — Melanokhyton**, meaning "black-cloaked," she moved silently through the night, **her presence felt more than seen**. The people of Thespiae held her in high esteem, believing that she watched over them as they slept, **her cloak a protective shroud against unseen dangers**.

The warriors of Thespiae, the **dark hoplites**, carried her essence into battle. **They donned armor adorned with symbols of the night**, invoking Nyx's power to cloak them from their enemies. *Picture these hoplites moving like shadows across the battlefield, their forms blending with the darkness, guided by the unseen hand of the goddess.* **They believed that under her mantle, they became one with the night**, gaining strength and stealth from her divine influence.

As a searcher, you might find that Nyx embodies the profound mysteries that lie within darkness. **She is not evil**, but rather represents the complexities and depths that are often misunderstood or overlooked. *Think of the quiet stillness of the night, when the world sleeps and dreams unfold — a time both serene and mysterious.* **Nyx invites you to explore these depths**, to find wisdom in the shadows and embrace the unknown aspects of your own nature.

In Greek mythology, while goddesses like Athena and Aphrodite are well-known, **the darker goddesses such as Nyx, Persephone, and Hekate offer deeper insights into the human psyche and the natural world**. They are often associated with mystery and darkness, which might make people think they're evil. However, as you've explored their stories in this chapter, it's clear that they aren't necessarily evil. **These Dark Goddesses**

are more complex than simple labels can convey. Their stories reveal Greek mythology's depth and intricacy, showing that terms like "dark" or "evil" are too simplistic to describe these multifaceted deities.

Nyx's influence is not only over the physical night but also over the transitions and transformations that occur within us. She governs the spaces between light and dark, consciousness and unconsciousness, life and death. **By embracing her, you may find guidance through your own periods of change**, drawing strength from the very shadows that once seemed daunting.

Imagine standing beneath a star-studded sky, the vast expanse of the universe above you. **In that moment, you might feel connected to Nyx**, the embodiment of the night, **a reminder of the endless possibilities that the darkness holds. She is the veil that both conceals and reveals**, inviting you to look beyond the surface and explore the depths of your own being.

Juno - Hera

Hera, the queen of the gods in Greek mythology, and her Roman counterpart, Juno, are often celebrated as goddesses of marriage and childbirth. **But as a searcher delving deeper into their stories, you uncover the darker facets of their divinity.**

Hera is not just the dignified wife of Zeus; **she embodies the fierce and unapologetic power of the divine feminine. Her wrath is legendary**, especially against those who betray her trust. When Zeus's infidelities result in offspring, **Hera's vengeance is swift and relentless.** *Think of how she tormented Hercules, sending serpents to his cradle and madness into his mind.* **These actions reveal a goddess who wields her power without hesitation**, demanding respect and loyalty.

While not directly associated with witchcraft, **Hera's profound influence and the secret rituals performed in her honor hint at a deeper, more mysterious aspect of her worship**. In certain regions, **women gathered in private ceremonies to invoke Hera's protection and guidance**, seeking to harness her strength in their own lives. **These rites, shrouded in mystery, allowed women to connect with the powerful energies Hera represents**.

Similarly, **Juno in Roman mythology holds a complex and multifaceted role. She is the protector of the state, the guardian of women, and a deity who can unleash formidable fury. Juno's darker side emerges in myths where she opposes heroes like Aeneas**, throwing obstacles in their paths to test their resolve. *Her relentless pursuit to hinder Aeneas's journey to Italy demonstrates her immense power and determination.*

Ancient Roman rituals often emphasized Juno's enigmatic aspects. Festivals like the **Matronalia** celebrated her as Juno Lucina, goddess of childbirth, but **there were also more**

secluded ceremonies where women sought her favor. These gatherings, veiled in secrecy, allowed women to honor Juno's strength and seek empowerment, though they were not explicitly linked to witchcraft.

Through these narratives, Hera and Juno emerge not only as goddesses of marriage and childbirth but as powerful figures embodying the darker, more complex aspects of womanhood. They represent the capacity for both creation and destruction, for nurturing and fiercely protecting what they hold dear.

As you explore their myths, you may find that Hera and Juno offer profound insights into embracing the full spectrum of the feminine divine. They remind you that strength, passion, and even righteous anger are integral parts of your inner goddess, waiting to be acknowledged and harnessed.

Diana and Artemis

Artemis, the goddess of the hunt, the wilderness, and the moon, moves silently through shadowed forests. **As a searcher**, you might sense her presence when the night air is cool and the moon hangs low in the sky. **She embodies the mystique of the wild and the untamed forces of nature**.

Artemis is not only a huntress but also **deeply connected to magic and witchcraft**. In the stillness of the night, **her influence over the arcane becomes most potent. She is often associated with the cycles of the moon**, which witches have long revered for their significance in magical practices.

In ancient times, **priestesses of Artemis would gather in secret groves**, performing rituals under the silver light of the moon. They sought her guidance, invoking her name to bless their spells and charms. **Her connection to magic is woven into the very fabric of her being**, tied to the mysteries of the moon and the hidden realms.

Artemis is a maiden goddess, embracing her independence and autonomy. **She represents the wild spirit**, free from constraints, roaming forests and mountains. This fierce independence is mirrored in her mastery over magic, unbound by societal norms or expectations. **She teaches you to trust your instincts**, to listen to the whispers of the natural world.

Consider the tale of Actaeon, a hunter who stumbled upon Artemis while she bathed in a secluded pool. Enraged by his intrusion, **she transformed him into a stag**, and he was torn apart by his own hounds. **This story illustrates her command over transformative magic**, a power that is both awe-inspiring and fearsome.

Her twin brother, Apollo, governs the sun, logic, and reason. In contrast, **Artemis governs the moon**, intuition, and the subconscious. **She guides you through the hidden landscapes of the psyche**, illuminating paths less traveled. **Her magic is subtle yet profound**, found in the rustling of leaves, the glow of fireflies, the quiet strength of the wilderness.

As you walk your path, **Artemis invites you to explore your own connection to magic. She encourages you to embrace your inner wildness**, to find power in solitude and communion with nature. **Her rites often involve rituals performed under the moonlight**, drawing upon lunar energies to manifest intentions and desires.

Across the cultures, **Diana mirrors Artemis's essence in Roman mythology. She is the goddess of the hunt, the moon, and childbirth. Diana's association with magic is equally profound**, and she holds a revered place among those who practice the ancient arts.

In the sacred woods of Nemi, **worshippers of Diana gathered in secret ceremonies. They called her Diana Nemorensis**, the goddess of the grove. **Her priestesses possessed great knowledge of herbs and healing**, using their skills to aid the sick and the needy. **Herbalism and magic were intertwined in Diana's domain**, reflecting the deep connection between the natural world and the mystical.

Diana is also linked to Hecate, the goddess of witchcraft and the crossroads. **In some traditions, they are seen as aspects of the same divine force**, representing different phases of the moon and facets of feminine power. **Diana's role as a lunar goddess places her firmly within the realm of magic**, where the moon's cycles influence the ebb and flow of energy.

The legend of Aradia tells of a woman sent by Diana to teach magic and witchcraft to the oppressed. **Aradia is portrayed as Diana's daughter**, a messenger who shares the secrets of the craft with humanity. **This tale highlights Diana's direct connection to the spread of magical knowledge**, positioning her as a central figure in the tradition of witchcraft.

As a searcher, you might feel drawn to the teachings of Artemis and Diana. **They offer guidance in embracing your own magical abilities**, encouraging you to find harmony with the natural world. **They symbolize the union of strength and intuition**, of action and reflection. **Their stories encourage you to seek balance**, to honor both the wildness within and the wisdom that comes from understanding the cycles of nature.

The phases of the moon play a crucial role in magic, and both goddesses are intimately connected to its rhythms. **The waxing moon is a time for growth and manifestation**, while **the waning moon supports release and introspection. By aligning your practices with these cycles**, you tap into the energies that Artemis and Diana govern.

In your journey, **you may feel the call to step into the moonlight**, to let the silver glow illuminate your path. **The magic of Artemis and Diana is not confined to ancient times; it resonates today**, inviting you to explore the mysteries that lie within and around you.

Envision standing beneath a full moon, the night sky stretching infinitely above. **You feel a connection to something greater**, a stirring of energies that flow through you and the world. **This is the realm of Artemis and Diana**, where magic is not just possible but natural.

They teach you to listen to the rustling of the leaves, to notice the subtle signs that guide you. **Magic, in their view, is about**

harmony with nature, about recognizing the interconnectedness of all things. **By honoring them, you honor the sacred within yourself**, unlocking the potential to weave magic into every aspect of your life.

Artemis and Diana stand as powerful embodiments of the divine feminine, representing independence, strength, and the profound depths of intuition. **Their connection to magic and witchcraft is a testament to the enduring power of these practices**, rooted in respect for the Earth and the cycles that govern it.

Their stories are not relics of the past but living inspirations, guiding you to embrace your own inner goddess. **As you walk your path, remember that the moonlight shining upon you is the same that illuminated the rites of ancient priestesses**, the same that continues to inspire seekers of wisdom and magic today.

Medusa the dark goddess of Athena

Medusa, with her serpentine hair and petrifying gaze, stands as one of the most enigmatic figures in Greek mythology. **As a searcher**, you might feel drawn to her story, sensing a deeper meaning beneath the surface. **She embodies the complex interplay between beauty and terror, vulnerability and power**.

Medusa was once a stunning maiden, her beauty unparalleled among mortals. **Her eyes sparkled like the deepest seas**, and **her hair flowed like silk under the sun**. Her radiance captivated all who beheld her, but it was this very beauty that led to her tragic transformation.

Athena, the goddess of wisdom and war, observed Medusa with a mix of admiration and concern. **In some tales, Medusa served as a priestess in Athena's temple**, dedicated to a life of purity and devotion. However, **an encounter between Medusa and Poseidon within the sacred temple** provoked Athena's wrath. **Feeling her sanctuary had been desecrated**, Athena directed her anger towards Medusa.

With a heavy heart, **Athena transformed Medusa into a Gorgon**, a creature with snakes for hair and a gaze that could turn anyone to stone. This transformation wasn't merely a punishment; **it was also a form of protection**. Medusa, once vulnerable, now possessed a power that made her untouchable. **Her beauty became a formidable shield**, deterring anyone who might seek to harm her.

The Gorgons, Medusa and her sisters Stheno and Euryale, lived at the edge of the world. **Their existence was cloaked in mystery**, symbolizing the unknown and feared aspects of the feminine divine. **They represent the shadows within**, the parts of ourselves we may hesitate to face.

Athena's role in Medusa's story reveals a darker facet of the goddess. **She is often seen as embodying reason and strategy**, yet here, **she acts out of anger and perhaps jealousy. This act showcases the duality within Athena**, reflecting both wisdom and vengeance.

Medusa becomes an extension of Athena, a manifestation of her suppressed emotions and the complexities of womanhood. **She is the shadow to Athena's light**, the raw emotion to Athena's calculated thought. This duality invites you to consider the multifaceted nature of the divine feminine within yourself.

Magic and witchcraft intertwine deeply with Medusa's narrative. Her very gaze is a potent spell, capable of petrifying those who dare to look upon her. **The snakes in her hair symbolize transformation and rebirth**, common themes in magical practices. *Consider the shedding of a snake's skin*, a renewal, much like **Medusa's own metamorphosis**.

In various traditions, **Medusa is revered as a protective figure. Amulets bearing her image, known as Gorgoneions, were used to ward off evil. Her visage, though fearsome, was a symbol of protection and power.** *Warriors might inscribe her likeness on their shields*, believing that **her terrifying appearance would repel enemies**.

The connection between Medusa and witchcraft lies in themes of transformation, protection, and embracing one's inner power. She represents the ability to harness personal trials and turn them into strength. Her story teaches you that even in the face of adversity, you can find empowerment.

Athena's involvement adds another layer. As a goddess of wisdom, she embodies knowledge, a key component of magical practice. **Her act of transforming Medusa can be seen as**

initiating Medusa into a new realm of existence, one where she wields immense power.

The Gorgons themselves are ancient symbols of the primal feminine force. They inhabit liminal spaces, the boundaries between the known and the unknown. **Their magic is raw and untamed**, much like the wild aspects of nature.

In exploring Medusa's story, **you confront themes of victimhood and empowerment**, injustice and retribution. **Her narrative challenges you to look beyond the surface**, to see the strength that can arise from hardship. **She invites you to embrace your own shadows**, to find the magic within the parts of yourself that society might overlook.

Medusa's legacy continues to inspire. Artists depict her not just as a monster, but as a symbol of feminine resilience and autonomy. **She embodies the transformative power of embracing one's true self**, with all its complexities.

As a searcher, you might feel a connection to Medusa's journey. **Her story resonates with anyone who has felt misunderstood or marginalized. She teaches that your power lies within**, waiting to be acknowledged and embraced.

Through the lens of magic and witchcraft, Medusa becomes a guide. **She shows you that the darkest moments can lead to profound personal growth. Her gaze, once feared, becomes a mirror**, reflecting the strength you possess.

In embracing Medusa, you also embrace the complexities of Athena. **You recognize that wisdom and emotion coexist**, that the divine feminine encompasses a spectrum of experiences. **Their intertwined stories offer a rich tapestry of lessons**, inviting you to delve deeper into your own psyche.

Medusa, the once-beautiful maiden transformed into a Gorgon, stands as a powerful symbol of transformation. **Her story is not solely one of tragedy**, but of reclamation and empowerment. **She embodies the magic that arises when you embrace all facets of yourself**, both light and dark.

Perhaps you might wear a token bearing her image, not as a symbol of fear, but as a reminder of your own resilience. **Let Medusa inspire you to face your own shadows**, to find strength in your experiences, and to harness the magic that lies within.

EGYPTIAN GODDESSES

When you think of ancient Egyptian deities, **perhaps only a few names come to mind**—figures like Ra, Isis, or Osiris. But **as a searcher delving deeper into the mysteries of the divine**, you uncover a pantheon rich with goddesses whose powers and stories have been waiting for you to discover. **Goddesses like Sekhmet, Nephthys, Hathor, and Nut**—the ancient Egyptian **Dark Goddesses**—await your exploration.

Sekhmet, the lioness goddess, stands at the crossroads of destruction and healing. **Her eyes blaze with the fire of the sun**, embodying the fierce and protective nature of the divine feminine. **Born from the eye of Ra**, she was sent to punish humanity for their transgressions. **Her rampage was so intense that it nearly annihilated mankind.** *But when the gods intervened, tricking her into drinking dyed beer thinking it was blood, she became intoxicated and her fury subsided.* **This transformation from wrath to calm reveals the duality within her**, showing you that **within your own anger lies the potential for profound healing**.

Nephthys, sister of Isis, dwells in the shadows. **She is the goddess of darkness, lamentation, and the unseen.** While Isis represents the bright aspects of magic and motherhood, **Nephthys embodies the hidden, the mysterious, the grieving. She stands by the bier of Osiris**, aiding in his resurrection. **Her role as protector of the dead connects you to the cycles of endings and beginnings. She invites you to explore the depths of your own shadow**, to find solace and wisdom in places others might fear. *In moments of loss, she whispers that grief is a pathway to deeper understanding.*

Hathor, often celebrated as the goddess of love, beauty, and joy, **harbors a darker aspect that is often overlooked. She transformed into Sekhmet**, becoming the instrument of divine punishment. **This shift reveals the complexity of her nature**, teaching you that **joy and rage can coexist within you. Hathor shows that embracing all parts of yourself leads to true harmony.** *When you feel conflicting emotions, she guides you to honor each feeling as a vital part of your being.*

Nut, the celestial goddess, arches her star-strewn body over the earth. **She is the embodiment of the night sky**, swallowing the sun each evening and giving birth to it each morning. **Her vast expanse represents the infinite possibilities of the universe. Nut governs the cycles of death and rebirth**, inviting you to look beyond the immediate and embrace the eternal. *Under a blanket of stars, you might feel her presence, a gentle reminder of the boundless potential within you.* **She encourages you to dream beyond limitations**, to see yourself as part of something greater.

As a searcher, you may feel the pull of these goddesses, sensing that **their ancient wisdom holds keys to unlocking your inner goddess. Their stories are not mere myths but echoes of truths within your own soul. They challenge you to face your fears**, to embrace both light and shadow within yourself. **Their power is not in being feared but in guiding you to your own strength.**

Perhaps you've felt Sekhmet's fierce courage when standing up for what you believe in, or **Nephthys's quiet comfort during times of sorrow.** *Maybe Hathor's duality resonates when you navigate complex emotions,* or **Nut's endless sky inspires you to reach for dreams you once thought impossible.**

Sekhmet

Sekhmet, whose name means **"One who is in control"** or **"She who is powerful,"** stands as one of the most formidable goddesses in ancient Egyptian mythology. **As a searcher delving into the depths of divine femininity**, you encounter Sekhmet not just as a deity but as a force of nature itself.

She is referred to as the **Mother Goddess**, embodying both human and animal forms. **Her depiction as a woman with the face of a lion** reflects her fierce and unyielding nature. Throughout ancient Egypt, sculptures, amulets, and monuments dedicated to Sekhmet attest to her immense significance.

Sekhmet is often considered a forgotten esoteric goddess. **Esoteric deities possess extraordinary abilities**, and yet, **she remains an enigma**. Not much is known about her compared to other deities; her stories are scarce, and she isn't mentioned as frequently in mythology. However, the few resources that do speak of her **praise her great but contradictory powers. She could bring disease, chaos, and death**, while also **administering healing and protection**.

Born from the fire in the eye of Ra, the sun god and creator of the universe, **Sekhmet was crafted as a weapon of vengeance**. In one legend, she is an incarnation of the sky goddess Hathor. After Ra created mankind, he observed them straying from the path of justice and order. Disappointed and angered, he decided to punish them. **From the fiery blaze of his eye, Sekhmet emerged**, earning the title **"The Eye of Ra." She was a manifestation of his power**, capable of breathing a fire hotter than the desert sun.

Sent to Earth to exact Ra's punishment, Sekhmet unleashed plagues across the lands. **Her fiery breath scorched everything**

in her path, killing almost all of mankind. **Her bloodlust was insatiable**, and none could halt her destruction. Witnessing the devastation, Ra regretted his decision.

He hadn't intended to annihilate humanity; he sought only to teach them a lesson. **If all mankind was destroyed, who would remain to learn?**

To stop her, Ra devised a plan. He commanded his priests to grind red ochre and mix it with beer. Under the cover of night, they poured this mixture over the land where Sekhmet slept. **When she awoke, she mistook the red beer for blood and drank it all. Intoxicated and pacified**, she fell into a deep sleep. Upon awakening, her rage subsided, **she returned to Ra**, and in some versions of the legend, he appointed her as the **goddess of war and chaos**.

Sekhmet's attributes are vast and complex.

She is the goddess of war, chaos, healing, plague, and the scorching desert sun. In the **Book of the Dead**, she is described as both a **destructive and creative force. She has the power to bring plagues upon mankind**, yet as a healing goddess, **she can be invoked to protect against diseases. There isn't a problem Sekhmet couldn't fix. She is the patron of healers and physicians**, and during wars, **she was the protector of the pharaohs**, leading them to victory.

She is known by thousands of names, each reflecting her multifaceted personality and powers.

Watcher and guardian of the West, Lady of the Mountains, Lady of the Flame, and **Mistress of Dread** are just a few. **Her epithets reveal her roles as both destroyer and protector**, emphasizing her dual nature.

Sekhmet is responsible for **bringing heat to the deserts**, earning her the name "**Nesert**," meaning flame. **She brings suffering and disease but only to those who anger her. She guards Ra and protects Ma'at**, the goddess of balance and justice. Because of her fierce and terrifying nature, **Sekhmet is called the "Lady of Terror."**

Her symbols include the **lioness**, representing her fierce strength; **red linen**, reflecting her bloodlust; the **sun disk**, signifying her connection to Ra; and **cats**, animals revered in Egyptian culture.

In ancient times, **everyone feared Sekhmet**, for she was the goddess of war.

However, **she is only threatening to those who disrespect her. She protected the ancient Egyptians by breathing fire and vanquishing their enemies**. Yet, when in battle, **Sekhmet could become blinded with rage**, destroying everything in her way. **Only drinking blood — or what she believed to be blood — could calm her fiery anger.**

If you wish to **appease Sekhmet**, you might **burn incense, play music**, or **offer her food and drink. Connecting with her requires respect and understanding of her dual nature**.

To seek her guidance, you could perform a meditation ritual:

Build an altar dedicated to Sekhmet, placing her images or symbols upon it. **Light candles**, their flames symbolizing her fiery essence. **Sit beside the altar**, closing your eyes, and **take deep breaths. Visualize Sekhmet**, allowing her presence to manifest. **Give yourself time**, and when you sense her or see her symbols, **ask her for guidance**.

As a searcher, reaching out to Sekhmet is not merely about seeking power but about embracing the **full spectrum of your inner strength.**

She teaches that within destruction lies the potential for healing, and within chaos, the opportunity for order. **By acknowledging both the fierce and nurturing aspects within yourself,** you **unlock the profound wisdom Sekhmet offers**.

In moments of anger or frustration, consider the lessons of Sekhmet. **Your passion can be a source of transformation**, both for yourself and those around you. **Harness it wisely**, and you, too, can become "**One who is in control.**"

Nephthys

Nephthys, one of the earliest Egyptian goddesses, was born from the union between the Sky and the Earth after **Ra** created the universe. **As a searcher**, you might be intrigued to know that **her Egyptian name is Nebthwt**, meaning "Mistress of the House" or "The Lady of the Temple."

In ancient myths, **Osiris**, the god of agriculture and fertility, and his wife **Isis**, the goddess of magic and light, ruled over mankind with justice and kindness. Their sister, **Nephthys**, was married to their brother **Set**, the god of war. Yet, **Nephthys harbored feelings for Osiris**. One day, **she transformed herself into Isis and seduced him**. They spent the night together, and from their union, **Anubis** was born.

When **Set discovered the betrayal**, he believed Osiris had seduced Nephthys. **Consumed by jealousy and hatred, Set plotted to murder his brother**. He succeeded, killing Osiris and taking the throne, with Nephthys by his side.

Isis was heartbroken over the loss of her husband. She searched tirelessly for his body, **hoping to bring him back to life so she could conceive his child**. Upon finding him, **she asked Nephthys to help protect his body from Set**. But **Set confronted Nephthys**, and under his wrath, **she revealed their hiding place. Set mutilated Osiris**, scattering his pieces across the land.

Overcome with guilt for betraying her sister, **Nephthys vowed to make amends**. Together, **the sisters searched for Osiris's scattered parts**, collecting them one by one. They **reassembled his body** and used their combined magic to bring him back to life. From this union, **Isis conceived a son, Horus**.

To protect her child from Set, **Isis hid Horus away. Nephthys, having learned from her mistakes, kept their secret.** She **nursed Horus and helped Isis raise him.** When Horus grew and reclaimed his rightful throne, **he honored Nephthys,** making her the head of his family and chief counselor. **Because of this, many Egyptians view Nephthys as a nurturing mother and a symbol of guidance and protection.**

Nephthys is often depicted as a woman with the symbol of her name atop her head. Her image adorned many ancient tombs, for **she protected the dead and attended to Osiris's mummification.** Associated with **darkness, twilight, and the setting sun, she transforms into a kite,** wailing to mourn the departed and **guarding the coffins and canopic jars** where the deceased's organs were stored.

Her symbols include **sycamore trees, temples, hawks, kites,** and even **beer. She is sometimes shown as a woman with wings,** emphasizing her protective nature.

As the Dark Goddess, Nephthys is the **goddess of death,** associated with decay and the transition to the afterlife. **She helps souls cross over,** caring for them even after they've departed. **She comforts grieving families,** assuring them their loved ones are safe. **This is why she is called the 'Friend of the Dead.'** In fact, **she is the only goddess who treats the dead with such love and kindness.**

Her followers often call upon her after a loved one's passing. **She is present during funerals,** guarding the dead. Nephthys possesses magical abilities akin to Isis. **Isis represents the force of light, while Nephthys embodies darkness — they balance each other.**

Interestingly, **Nephthys also became the goddess of birth after giving birth to Anubis,** the god of death. This duality highlights her role in both beginnings and endings.

To connect with Nephthys, you might perform a visualization ritual. **Find a quiet space and sit comfortably. Close your eyes, place your hands over your heart,** and **take a deep breath.** Visualize **the light of Nephthys flowing through every part of your body. Exhale and feel her light grounding you,** extending beneath your feet. **Inhale again, filling your heart with her essence. Whisper her name,** allowing her light to fill your space. If you sense her presence, **ask her any questions that rest upon your heart.** When you're ready, **express your gratitude** for her guidance.

As a searcher, embracing Nephthys's wisdom can lead you to deeper understanding and inner peace. **She teaches that in darkness, there is comfort,** and that endings are but beginnings in disguise.

Hathor

Hathor, closely associated with **Sekhmet**, holds a unique place in ancient Egyptian mythology. Some historians believe that **Sekhmet is derived from Hathor**. She is depicted either as a cow or a woman with a cow's head. **As a searcher**, you might find her dual nature intriguing. **Hathor is the daughter of Ra** and was highly venerated among the ancient Egyptians. **Her name means "Temple of Horus,"** referring to the myth where **Horus (the sun god) enters her mouth every night to rest and is reborn each morning to light the sky**. This story explains the daily journey of the sun.

Hathor was once an image of love and kindness, but she had a much darker side in earlier times. In some legends, **Ra sent Hathor to punish mankind for their disobedience. She unleashed her vengeance, destroying everything and everyone**. Her wrath was so immense that it transformed her into **Sekhmet**. After her rampage, when she finally calmed down, **she returned to being Hathor**, but she had changed. **She became a better, kinder, and calmer version of herself**.

The goddess who once sought to annihilate the world **became an ally to mankind. She blessed them with many gifts and helped the less fortunate**. Whenever they prayed to her, **she answered their calls. She became the mother goddess**, and many other goddesses are believed to be her avatars.

In another myth, when **Horus** grew up, he sought to claim the throne from his uncle **Set**. Set was cunning and untrustworthy. **Horus took his case to the council of gods**, led by **Ra**. However, **Ra became angry and refused to participate in the trial**, causing great concern among the gods.

Hathor knew that her father's anger could bring about the end of the world. Determined to restore balance, she visited Ra. In an unexpected move, she danced before him and used her charm to amuse him. Her actions delighted Ra, and his anger subsided. He returned to the council to handle Horus's case.

This story highlights the significance of masculinity and femininity. When both are in harmony, they bring balance to the universe.

Hathor is the goddess of love, celebration, music, dance, motherhood, gratitude, intoxication, and joy, similar to Venus and Aphrodite from Roman and Greek mythology. She is the patron of women and their health. She is also the ruler of childbirth, the East, the West, fertility, agriculture, the moon, the sun, and the sky.

Hathor has many roles. She renews the cosmos, helps women give birth, and resurrects the dead. As a lunar deity, she guides boats at night until they reach the shore safely. In ancient Egypt, night was a metaphor for death, so it is believed that she illuminates the way for the deceased to reach their final resting place.

Her symbols include the cow, cow's ears, cow horns, solar disk, papyrus plant, sycamore tree, serpent, and lioness.

Hathor holds the great honor of being the goddess of the afterlife in the Field of Reeds. This place is similar to the concept of paradise, where the dead spend eternity with their loved ones without pain or suffering. When a good woman or girl dies, she assumes the likeness of Hathor before crossing to the Field of Reeds.

To connect with Hathor, you might offer roses, cedar, cinnamon, myrrh, wine, beer, butter, cheese, bread, dates, figs, freshwater, jasmine, chamomile, or rose oil, perfumes, gold, or copper.

Setting up a simple altar in her honor, with a picture or statue of her and a red or white candle, can be a meaningful gesture.

As a searcher, embracing Hathor's story can unlock a deeper understanding of the balance between light and darkness within yourself. **She teaches that transformation is possible**, and that from chaos can come kindness and joy. **By connecting with her, you may find guidance in your own journey towards harmony and self-discovery**.

Nut

Nut, daughter of **Shu**, the god of air, and **Tefnut**, the goddess of rainfall and moisture, stands as one of the most significant deities in ancient Egyptian mythology. **As a searcher**, you might be intrigued to know that she is **Ra's granddaughter** and married to **Geb**, the god of the earth. **Nut** is the **goddess of the sky**, and her name means **"water,"** often depicted with a water pot on her head.

When **Ra** created **Nut** (the sky) and **Geb** (the earth), **they were inseparable**, their love so profound that **they embraced endlessly. Their closeness prevented Nut from bearing children. Shu**, Nut's father, desired grandchildren and grew jealous of their unbroken union. **He forced them apart**, creating the separation between the sky and the earth as we know it. *The longing between Nut and Geb was so intense that even today, the sky arches over the earth, yearning to reunite.*

In another tale, **Ra loved Nut and wished to make her his wife**. However, **she was in love with Geb**, and they were already together. **When Ra discovered their secret union**, he was furious. **He cursed Nut so she could never have children in any month of the year.** Desperate to break the curse, **Nut sought help from Thoth**, the god of wisdom. **Moved by her plight**, Thoth devised a clever plan. He challenged **Khonsu**, the moon god, to a game of checkers. With each victory, **Thoth won a portion of moonlight**, and eventually, he accumulated enough to create **five extra days** beyond the existing calendar. **Since these days were not part of any month, Nut was able to bear children**, giving birth to **Osiris, Isis, Seth**, and **Nephthys**.

Nut also played a vital role in **helping Ra ascend to the sky. Ra decided to abdicate his throne and retire to the heavens, but he**

was old and weak. **Nun**, the primordial waters, asked **Nut** to carry **Ra** on her back. Doubting her ability, **Nut** hesitated, but **Nun transformed her into a cow**, granting her the strength needed. **Ra rode upon Nut**, and together they ascended, establishing **Ra's place in the skies**.

Nut is often depicted as a **beautiful naked woman with wings**, arching over the earth, her body adorned with stars. **She protects the world from Nun**, the chaotic waters of creation, and is credited with giving birth to key deities of the Great Ennead, including **Ra, Shu, Tefnut, Geb, Osiris, Isis, Seth**, and **Nephthys**. Initially the **goddess of the night sky**, associated with the **Milky Way, her role expanded over time**, and she became the **goddess of all skies**.

Her symbols include the **sky, cow, stars**, and concepts like **freedom, wisdom, abundance, eternity**, and **immortality**. Animals like **frogs, bunnies**, and **bees**, and elements like **lotus flowers**, and gemstones such as **opal, blue topaz, tourmaline**, and **sapphire** are connected to her. **Colors like blue and black** represent her essence.

As a Dark Goddess, Nut is the guardian of sarcophagi and coffins. She watches over the dead, guiding them until their rebirth in the afterlife.

To invoke **Nut**, you might choose a place outdoors under the night sky, or set up an indoor altar adorned with symbols of the night like stars or the moon. **Light a white or blue candle**, place her symbols on the altar, and make an offering. **Sit quietly**, focusing on your breath. **Clear your mind and visualize Nut. Ask her for guidance**, and be open to receiving her wisdom.

In **Kemetic spirituality**, a belief system inspired by ancient Egyptian religion, **Nut's cycle embodies the circle of life. Every night, she swallows the sun god, and gives birth to him each** morning. **She also swallows the moon every morning,** giving birth to her at night. This eternal cycle reflects the belief that **the universe is an extension of yourself.**

The **dark ancient Egyptian goddesses** like **Nut** embody a multitude of characteristics. **They can be both bloodthirsty forces of destruction and compassionate guides and protectors. They represent the complex, multifaceted nature of ancient Egyptian mythology,** where light and darkness, creation and destruction, intertwine in a cosmic tapestry.

MESOPOTAMIAN GODDESSES

You step into the ancient lands of Mesopotamia, where the veils between worlds are thin and whispers of forgotten goddesses echo in the shadows. **Ereshkigal**, **Lilith**, and **Inanna** await you, each holding secrets of the divine feminine that resonate deep within your soul.

As **a searcher** seeking inner grounding, you find yourself drawn to their stories, their mysteries entwined with your own journey. **Their myths are not just tales of old but mirrors reflecting the hidden facets of your being**.

Ereshkigal, the enigmatic queen of the underworld, **beckons you into the depths of transformation**. She rules over the realm where souls confront their deepest truths. *In moments when you face your shadows, Ereshkigal's presence is there, guiding you through the darkness*. **Her story teaches that embracing the unknown can lead to profound rebirth**.

Lilith, shrouded in mystery and often misunderstood, embodies **the fierce independence and untamed spirit** that **stirs within you. She is the embodiment of autonomy**, refusing to be subdued or silenced. *When you assert your boundaries and honor your true desires, you walk alongside Lilith*. **Her tale encourages you to embrace your authentic self without apology**.

Inanna, goddess of love and war, **navigates the delicate balance between polarities. Her descent into the underworld and triumphant return** symbolize the cycles of loss and renewal that **you experience in your own life**. *In times of hardship and*

resurgence, Inanna's journey mirrors your path toward wholeness.
**She invites you to find strength in vulnerability and wisdom
in adversity.**

Through their legends, **you uncover the multifaceted nature of
the divine feminine. These Dark Goddesses are not confined
to darkness alone but encompass the full spectrum of
existence. They hold the keys to understanding the
complexities within you,** illuminating both shadow and light.

**By delving into their myths, roles, and qualities, you forge a
connection with these powerful archetypes. Their symbols
resonate with your inner world,** offering insights and guidance.
*A nocturnal owl may remind you of Lilith's wisdom, a starry night sky
might echo Ereshkigal's domain, a blooming rose could symbolize
Inanna's duality.*

**This chapter invites you to journey with Ereshkigal, Lilith, and
Inanna,** exploring the depths of their stories and discovering **the
reflections of your own inner goddess. As you embrace their
wisdom, you may find the grounding and empowerment you
seek.**

Lilith

Also known as Lillake, Lilitu, Belili, and Baalat, Lilith weaves her presence through numerous cultures and traditions. As a searcher, you may feel her enigmatic energy calling to a deep part of your soul.

In Jewish mythology, **she emerges as Adam's first wife**, a woman created equally from the same earth. **Lilith refused to submit to her husband's wishes**, believing in mutual respect and equality. **Choosing freedom over subservience, she left Eden**, and some tales whisper that she transformed into a serpent, leading to Adam and Eve's exile. **Her story reflects the courage to stand firm in one's beliefs**, even when it leads to isolation.

Yet **her origins trace back further**, to the Sumero-Babylonian goddess with similar dark and spirited qualities. **Lilith is depicted as a nocturnal being**, sometimes accompanied by an owl or transforming into one. **She lurks in the shadows of the night**, a symbol of mystery and the untamed feminine. *Her inability to bear children in certain legends fuels her anguish, leading her to acts of vengeance.* **In contrast, the Canaanites revered her as the "Divine Lady"**, highlighting her multifaceted nature.

One of her earliest mentions is on a clay tablet from Ur, dating back to 2000 B.C., but **her essence stretches back to Sumer around 3000 B.C.** In Babylonian legends, **she is the Maid of Desolation**, a figure both feared and admired. **Despite her demon-like features—claws and bird feet—she possesses an enchanting beauty.** *No man who encounters her can resist her allure.* In rituals, **Lilith is represented by red jasper, garnet, or carnelian**, stones that **convey passion and sensuality**.

In a Sumerian legend, **Lilith's jealousy of Inanna**, the goddess of war and love, **leads her to inhabit a sacred tree** that Inanna intends to make her throne. **In bird form, Lilith perches upon the tree**, preventing Inanna from claiming it. *Some say this act was a deliberate attempt to hinder Inanna's rise to power.* **But when the hero Gilgamesh intervenes, Lilith flees**, allowing Inanna to assume her rightful place.

Her association with breasts in ancient Mesopotamian culture ties to her sexual symbolism. Lilith is said to cause illnesses in women, hindering them from breastfeeding and causing their children to suffer. *This perhaps mirrors her own pain and a desire to prevent others from experiencing what she cannot.*

As an empowering Dark Goddess, Lilith embodies Wild Freedom. She teaches you to embrace who you truly are, trusting that those meant to accept you will find their way into your life. **She encourages self-sovereignty**, even when society shames or casts you aside for your thoughts, feelings, or actions. **No outside validation is worth sacrificing your inner truth or abandoning the love you have for yourself.**

Lilith urges you not to submit blindly to others' wills and needs. Instead, **she inspires you to uplift those marginalized by society**, to **devote yourself to a fierce passion that supports your tender qualities** rather than suppressing them. **Working with Lilith can bring you closer to the divine feminine archetype you identify with**, empowering you to stand in your own light.

At the same time, **she doesn't advocate for ignoring your loved ones' needs. Lilith fosters raising your standards**, finding ways to honor others' demands while also tending to your own. **She guides you in nurturing the seed of your inner wisdom**, allowing your values to blossom in a diverse world. **She acknowledges that conflicted feelings about meeting others'** needs may stem from an inner void, but **embracing this can lead to profound personal growth.**

This dark aspect of Lilith may seem dangerous and intense, but **it holds the potential for balance. She can challenge you,** prompting you to confront conflicts, irritation, or selfish tendencies. *In modern terms, she can reflect the shadow side we all possess.* **With awareness and caution, you can navigate these energies,** harnessing her power for positive transformation.

Across cultures, whether seen as a blend of light and dark or entirely dark, Lilith offers liberation to those she encounters. By embracing her lessons, you tap into a sense of uninhibited freedom, shedding constraints that no longer serve you. While some may view her methods as radical, **they can be necessary to face truths we might otherwise avoid.**

Lilith stands as a powerful archetype, inviting you to delve into the depths of your being. **She challenges you to embrace all facets of yourself**, both shadow and light, **unlocking the wild freedom within.**

Inanna

Known by the Sumerians as "the lady of the heavens," Inanna stands as one of the most complex and mysterious dark deities. As a searcher, you may feel the pull of her dual nature, which embodies both fierce power and deep vulnerability. Inanna's energy flows between light and dark, between the upper world and the underworld, challenging you to explore the hidden parts of yourself.

Inanna is thought to be the daughter of **Ningal** and **Anu**, and the twin sister of **Ereshkigal**, another dark goddess in Mesopotamian mythology. **Her story is a web of contradictions**. In some myths, **Inanna is pushed into an arranged marriage with Dumuzi**, the shepherd god. In others, Dumuzi is merely her consort, a passing lover in her endless journey toward self-mastery. **Either way, Inanna fiercely maintains her boundaries**, resisting the idea that her desires can be controlled by another. This contrasts with her portrayal in the *Epic of Gilgamesh*, where she pursues the hero with a tempestuous lust and is rejected, a rejection that further reveals the complexity of her character.

Her traits shift like the phases of the moon. On one side, **Inanna is an ambitious and empowering goddess**, a ruler with influence and a thirst for conquest. On the other, **she is seen as a shy maiden, her freedom restricted by the society that surrounds her. Her sensuality is a core theme throughout her stories**, a raw expression of her divine power. **In the hearts of her followers, Inanna is prayed to for help with unrequited love and impotence.** *Some even claim she was the patron of the "ladies of the night," a protector of the forgotten and the unloved.*

She is often depicted in contrasting forms. In art, **Inanna may appear nude**, her figure revealing the vulnerability beneath her power. In other images, **she wears armor, a warrior with weapons at her side**, ready to defend what is hers. In some depictions, she even **wears a beard**, claiming the masculine force needed to command respect and authority in battle. This duality speaks to the core of her nature—**a goddess who can be both fierce and nurturing, a bringer of life and a harbinger of death.**

Inanna's connection to the underworld is one of the most significant stories that define her as a Dark Goddess. In her descent, she is stripped of everything—her power, her beauty, her very identity. At each of the seven gates of the underworld, she surrenders more of herself, layer by layer, until she stands naked before her sister, **Ereshkigal**. Here, she faces the deepest darkness, the ultimate confrontation with her own mortality and ego.

In one version of the myth, **Inanna's descent is a gesture of reconciliation**, a desire to mend the rift between her and her twin. Yet **Ereshkigal, grieving the death of her husband, is not in a forgiving mood**. *In fact, some say it was Inanna's actions that caused her husband's death.* The sisters, bound by blood yet separated by their realms, are unable to heal their wounds. **Ereshkigal leaves Inanna to die**, hanging her body on a hook, lifeless and powerless.

But **Inanna's story doesn't end in death**. With the help of her loyal servant, **Ninšubur**, and the god **Enki**, she is revived— *reborn through the red waters of life.* She emerges from the underworld, transformed, with more power than before. **This journey mirrors the journey many of us must take when we confront the darkest parts of ourselves**. It is not a path of simple introspection but one of total surrender, stripping away the illusions that have shielded us from our shadow.

As **a searcher**, you are invited to take your own "Underworld Journey." **Inanna encourages you to explore the hidden,**

repressed parts of yourself that you might fear or deny. *These are not places of simple answers, but deep, often painful realizations.* Inanna shows that it is only by confronting this darkness that true empowerment can emerge. **Like her, you may find that your journey leads to the death of the ego**, but from that death, new life, and understanding bloom.

This journey is not for the faint of heart. It requires the courage to surrender to the unknown, to strip away all that keeps your ego intact, and to face the raw truth of who you are beneath it all. **Inanna's myth teaches that the layers we wear to protect ourselves can also keep us trapped**. In confronting the shadow, you are not weakened; instead, **you gain the strength to heal and grow**, uncovering the grief, shame, guilt, and denial that have held you back.

Inanna emerged from her descent with greater power and insight, reclaiming her title among the living and the dead. She became **the goddess of transformation**, and her journey mirrors the cycles we go through in our own lives. **As a Dark Goddess, she teaches that the darkest parts of ourselves hold the keys to our true strength. Her power lies in embracing the whole self — the light and the dark, the vulnerability and the fierceness, the love and the anger**.

By working with Inanna, **you too can find the courage to descend into your inner darkness**, to confront the parts of yourself that may seem too difficult to face. And like her, **you will rise again**, transformed, stronger, and more whole than before.

Ereshkigal

Ereshkigal, the Queen of the Underworld, moves through the shadows with quiet authority, her presence both feared and revered in ancient Mesopotamian mythology. **As a searcher**, you may feel her energy stir in the deepest parts of your soul, where the weight of unspoken fears and unhealed wounds lies. She is not a figure you seek out lightly, but once her call is heard, it is impossible to ignore.

Her name, **Ereshkigal**, translates to "Queen of the Great Below." **She rules the land of the dead, a place where souls eat dust and drink mud**. Her palace, **Ganzir**, is said to be built of **lapis lazuli**, a place of allure and danger, where souls are drawn into her realm but never return. **Ereshkigal holds the souls close, refusing to release them**, a gatekeeper of mysteries that mortals fear to uncover. **Her seven gates guard the way to the underworld**, each one stripping away more of those who pass through. Her role as the sole ruler of this dark kingdom was only shared when she took **Nergal** as her consort, a deity who helped her govern the realm of the dead.

But beyond her role as the queen of the dead, **Ereshkigal is a force of transformation**, embodying the journey through death, grief, and loss to emerge into something more powerful. Her power lies not only in ruling the underworld but in **guiding those who dare to confront the darkness within themselves**. *She is the whisper in your ear, urging you to look inward, to face the pain you have hidden away, and to acknowledge the grief that lingers in your shadow.*

Ereshkigal's presence is felt most strongly in the myth of Inanna's descent. While her sister, **Inanna**, shines in the upper world, Ereshkigal rules below in solitude. When Inanna descends to her, seeking to claim the throne of the underworld, **Ereshkigal does not welcome her with open arms**. Instead, she strips Inanna of everything, leaving her exposed and vulnerable. **This is the essence of Ereshkigal's power** — to **strip away the layers we hide behind,** forcing us to confront what lies beneath. *Only by surrendering to the pain, to the loss of control, can true transformation begin.*

Though feared, **Ereshkigal is also respected**, especially for her dark sensuality. In ancient depictions, **she is shown as a winged naked woman**, surrounded by symbols of power — owls, lions, and snakes. Her feet are talons, and she stands atop lions, embodying the wild and untamed forces of the underworld. **She is primal, raw, and unapologetically herself**, a reminder that there is power in embracing the parts of ourselves that society may deem too wild or too dark. *Her wings are pointed downward, grounding her in the realm of the dead, but her power rises like a tide within.*

As **a Dark Goddess**, Ereshkigal calls you to journey into your own underworld, to face the shadows of your past, your pain, your deepest fears. **She teaches that grief and pain are not to be banished quickly** but are to be **held with compassion, processed slowly, and transformed into power. Quick fixes don't serve you here**. Ereshkigal teaches that **the process of healing requires patience, love, and understanding**, not avoidance. *Pain, when embraced, can become the foundation of your rebirth.*

Many who work with **Ereshkigal find her to be an empowering force during times of deep transformation**. She is particularly potent for those engaging in ancestral healing or exploring long-buried emotions. *She teaches you to nurture your pain*, to see it not as a burden but as a source of strength that, when integrated, can lead to profound growth. **What you project outwardly as fear,** anger, or sorrow is merely a reflection of the pain within. By embracing that pain, you learn how to reclaim your power and transform it into something healing and life-giving.

Ereshkigal holds the key to your liberation. She demands that you face your fears, one by one, to confront the grief, the uncertainty, and the shadows that haunt you. Only then can you truly be free—free of the burdens that weigh you down, free of the masks you wear, and free to live fully in your truth. *Her teachings show you that the fear of facing your pain is far greater than the pain itself.* By opening yourself to the darkness, you find that it will not consume you. Even if it feels like dying a thousand deaths, you will emerge, as Ereshkigal herself did, reborn with clarity and strength.

This goddess of the underworld reminds you that sovereignty comes from within. To reclaim your life, you must first reclaim your shadow, honoring it with the same reverence you give your light. Ereshkigal stands beside you in this journey, offering the power to heal and the strength to face whatever comes.

SLAVIC GODDESS

Ancient Slavic lore whispers through the ages, elusive and mysterious, with fragments scattered like forgotten memories. **As a searcher**, you may feel the pull of this hidden world, a place where the veil between the living and the spiritual is thin, and the old gods still linger in the shadows. **Slavic mythology is a puzzle for historians**, as there are no original written records of the deities, rituals, or stories that shaped the beliefs of the ancient Slavs. **What we know now comes from those who came later** — monks and chroniclers who captured these stories during the Christianization of the region.

Yet, **these tales are far older than the records suggest**, with roots that some researchers trace back to the Proto-Indo-European era, and perhaps even to the Neolithic period. **The Slavs were not one unified group**, but a collection of tribes, each with its own gods, rituals, and myths. Their stories were passed down through generations, shaped by the land and the people who called it home. In the East, the Slavs' beliefs intertwined with those of the ancient Iranians, their gods sharing traits and powers.

By the late 12th century, the ancient Slavic traditions were in their final days. **Bishop Absalon and his Danish forces invaded**, and with the destruction of the statue of **Svantevit**, the god of war and abundance, **a door closed on Slavic paganism**. The old ways were replaced by Christianity, and the gods and goddesses of the Slavic pantheon were forgotten by most.

But **not all of them faded away. Some linger in the shadows**, their stories and powers still alive in the hearts of those who remember. **Among these forgotten figures stand two powerful, dark female deities — Baba Yaga** and **Marzanna. These goddesses are often misunderstood**, their true nature obscured by time and later interpretations. But in their stories, there is power, mystery, and a deep connection to the cycles of life, death, and rebirth.

Baba Yaga, perhaps the most famous of the Slavic goddesses, is a figure of both terror and wisdom. **She lives deep in the forest**, her house perched on chicken legs, always turning to face those who seek her. **Her nature is ambiguous**, as she is both a bringer of death and a giver of life. To those who enter her realm, she offers riddles and challenges, forcing them to confront their deepest fears. *Some who seek her wisdom find it, but only after paying a price.* **Baba Yaga teaches that wisdom comes not from safety, but from risk, and that to grow, one must face the darkness.**

In Slavic stories, **she is often depicted as an old crone**, haggard and bent, but her power is immense. **She represents the wildness of the natural world**, untamed and unpredictable. **She embodies the cycles of death and rebirth**, much like the changing seasons. Those who understand her, who approach her with respect, may leave her forest changed — stronger, wiser, and more grounded. *But for those who seek to trick her or use her power selfishly, Baba Yaga has no mercy.*

Marzanna, on the other hand, is the goddess of winter and death. **Her story is intertwined with the turning of the seasons.** Each year, as winter descends, **Marzanna's cold grip tightens on the land**, symbolizing the death of the old year and the approach of darkness. **She represents the inevitable end**, the part of the cycle that must come before renewal. In ancient Slavic tradition, she was honored with rituals at the end of winter. *Villages would create an effigy of Marzanna*, which they would then burn or drown, symbolically ending winter and welcoming the arrival of spring.

But **Marzanna is more than a bringer of death. She is also a symbol of transformation.** Her presence reminds us that endings are not final but are a necessary part of the cycle of life. **In her cold, there is a quiet power**, the stillness that comes before new life begins. **To work with Marzanna is to confront your own endings**, to understand that every loss, every death, is followed by rebirth. *It is only by embracing the cold and the dark that we can truly appreciate the warmth and light that follow.*

Both Baba Yaga and Marzanna represent powerful aspects of the dark feminine. They are not easily understood, nor are they meant to be. They challenge you, as a searcher, to confront the parts of yourself that are hidden or feared. They ask you to walk into the forest, to feel the chill of winter, and to face the shadow. **It is only by doing so that you can unlock the deeper parts of your being,** the parts that have been waiting for you to notice them.

Their stories are not just tales of old, but guides for your own journey. Baba Yaga and Marzanna remind you that life is full of cycles, of endings and beginnings, of death and rebirth. **By embracing both the light and the dark**, you become whole, grounded, and in tune with the natural flow of the world.

Baba yaga

Baba Yaga, the ancient deity of old bones, emerges from the depths of **Slavic folklore** as a figure of both fear and fascination. **As a searcher**, you may be drawn to her mysterious and complex nature, one that resists clear definitions. Known as a **notorious witch**, Baba Yaga resides deep within the vast, untamed forest in a mystical hut, her power intertwined with the shadows of the unknown.

Though feared for her reputation of **imprisoning and consuming her victims**, especially children, **Baba Yaga's presence carries deeper meaning**. She is more than a witch of darkness; **she is a symbol of female empowerment** and transformation. Her connection to the **Water of Life**, a mystical liquid capable of resurrecting the dead, reveals her role as both a destroyer and a giver of life. *To approach Baba Yaga is to confront the raw forces of death and rebirth within yourself.*

The true meaning of **"Baba Yaga"** remains elusive, adding to the mystique surrounding her. **"Baba"** is commonly understood to mean **"old woman"** or **"grandmother"**, and it's still used in countries like Bulgaria and Serbia to refer to older women. But the word **"Yaga"** is a puzzle, its origins unclear. Some believe it may derive from words in other **Slavic languages**, such as **"jeza,"** meaning horror or anger, or **"jedza,"** meaning witch. While her name and origins are shrouded in mystery, **her presence in Slavic culture is undeniable**. *She existed long before written records, a force passed down through the oral tradition.*

In the old tales, **Baba Yaga is depicted as a terrifying figure** — sharp iron teeth, a long, bony body, and a nose so pointed it nearly touches the ceiling of her hut. **Her legs are thin and made of clay**, and she is stripped of all femininity, engaging in activities that defy the conventions of womanhood. Unlike the stereotypical witch flying on a broomstick, **Baba Yaga travels in a mortar**—an instrument traditionally used by women for grinding flax and spinning cloth, **symbols of birth, creation, and death**. She rows with a pestle and sweeps away her tracks with a broom, always moving forward, always erasing the past. *Her journey is symbolic of the endless cycle of life and death.*

But Baba Yaga is much more than the stories tell. While many fear her for her chaotic and unpredictable nature, **she is a guardian of deep, ancient wisdom**. *To seek her out is to step into the unknown, to be willing to risk everything for transformation.* Those who dare enter her forest are tested, challenged to prove their worth. If they succeed, **Baba Yaga may grant them the help they seek**. If they fail, she shows no mercy.

Her **hut**, an iconic image in Slavic folklore, is as enchanted as she is. **It stands on massive chicken legs**, allowing it to move freely through the forest, **searching for those in need of Baba Yaga's guidance**. The hut groans and creaks with each step, its very structure alive, surrounded by human bones and skulls—a clear warning of the danger within. Yet **the house itself has its own soul**, a reflection of the wild, untamed forces that Baba Yaga embodies. The human skulls around the hut are not merely symbols of death but reminders of the life and transformation that always follow.

Baba Yaga is part of a greater archetype—along with her two sisters, who share her name and power. Together, **they represent the triple goddess**: maiden, mother, and crone. **Baba Yaga is the crone**, the wise and terrifying figure who oversees the transition between life and death. She holds the knowledge of the **Water of Life and Death**, capable of healing wounds with one hand and bringing the dead back to life with the other. **In her oven**, a symbol of both the womb and the earth, Baba Yaga carries the power of creation and destruction, birth and death. **Her fire burns fiercely**, but it also gives life, a paradox that defines her existence.

In the stories, Baba Yaga doesn't seek out her victims. She is not driven by a need to conquer or destroy, like many other villains in folklore. **She waits for those who seek her**, and when they come, she tests them. **Her motives are neutral**, neither good nor evil. She is a force of nature, as unpredictable as a storm. If you approach her with respect and courage, **she may grant you the transformation you seek**. But if you fail her tests, **you will face the full wrath of her chaotic power**.

Her neutrality is what makes Baba Yaga so powerful and real. She doesn't operate by a moral code, and she doesn't care to be understood. **She exists as a figure of transformation**, guiding those who come to her through their journey, whether they realize it or not. *In this way, she represents the wild, untamed forces within us*, the parts that are not bound by society's rules or expectations.

One of Baba Yaga's most famous appearances is in the story of **Vasilissa the Beautiful**. Sent to Baba Yaga's forest by her cruel stepmother, Vasilissa undergoes a series of tests that challenge her strength, wit, and resilience. **Baba Yaga grants her the fire she seeks**, but not without exacting a heavy price. The fire burns Vasilissa's cruel family to ashes, a symbol of the destructive power that comes with transformation. Yet, in the end, **Vasilissa emerges stronger, reborn through her trials**.

In another tale, **The Frog Princess**, a prince marries a frog who later reveals herself to be a beautiful woman. **Baba Yaga plays a pivotal role in his quest to win her back after he betrays her trust**, testing the prince and guiding him toward the transformation he needs to become worthy of his bride once more.

Baba Yaga is a goddess of transformation. She offers the path of change, but it is not without risk. **To work with her, you must be prepared to confront the parts of yourself that you fear most**. She will not let you hide, nor will she comfort you as you pass through the trials she sets before you. **But if you succeed, you will emerge stronger, more grounded, and more in touch with your true self**. *Her lessons are hard, but they are necessary for those seeking inner grounding and empowerment.*

In Baba Yaga's world, you are called to face the wild, untamed parts of yourself, to embrace the darkness and uncertainty that comes with transformation. **Only then can you access the deeper wisdom she offers**, and only then can you find the path to reclaiming your power.

Marzanna

Marzanna, the **Goddess of Winter and Death**, carries with her the cold grip of the underworld, and her name is whispered in many forms—**Morana**, **Marzena**, and **Morena**. She is the dark counterpart to **Ceres**, the Roman goddess of agriculture, and **Hecate**, the Greek goddess of witchcraft and night. Marzanna's presence extends far beyond the barren fields of winter. **As a wayfarer**, seeking answers in the shadows, you may find that her cold, mysterious power touches something deeper within you.

In Slavic mythology, **Marzanna is not just the goddess of winter**, but she embodies the cyclical nature of life and death. Her story is one of transformation, rebirth, and the delicate balance between destruction and creation. Once, she was a goddess of nature, tied to the fertile earth. **But betrayal turned her heart to ice**, and winter became her domain.

The legend of **Marzanna's marriage to Jarylo**, the god of spring and war, speaks to the eternal dance between life and death. Marzanna, the daughter of **Mokosz**, the great mother, and **Perun**, the god of thunder, was once aligned with the forces of life. When Jarylo, her twin brother, was stolen away to the underworld as a child, neither knew the truth of their relationship. Upon his return, they fell in love, unaware of their shared blood. **Their union brought balance to the world**, restoring the natural cycles of life and death, growth and decay. But as with all things, this harmony was fleeting. When Jarylo betrayed her, **Marzanna killed him in a rage**, marking the end of the fertile season and the arrival of winter's chill.

Her grief and anger, the weight of betrayal, transformed her into **the cold, feared deity of death**. In her fury, she brought winter to the land, her icy breath suffocating the warmth of life. **When Jarylo's death coincides with the fall**, it ushers in the long, dark winter months. Yet, each spring, **Dziewanna, the goddess of spring, kills Marzanna**, allowing Jarylo to rise once more, only to be felled again with each changing season. Their tragic dance of love and death **marks the rhythm of the seasons**, ensuring that neither life nor death can reign supreme forever.

In this way, **Marzanna's story is not merely one of death**, but of renewal, of the cycles that turn endlessly within the world and within ourselves. Her presence serves as a reminder that death is not an end but a transformation, **a part of the greater cycle of existence**.

Her name, **Marzanna**, comes from the ancient word for death. It ties her to **Mars**, the Roman god of war, and to the Russian word for pestilence. Death, war, destruction—these are her domains. Yet, there is something more beneath the surface. As you explore her deeper layers, **you will find that winter, though harsh, is necessary**. It allows for stillness, for reflection, and for the preparation of the new growth that follows.

Marzanna's role as the **harbinger of winter** is reflected in the fear she evokes. **Winter brings with it death**—not just of the crops and the trees but of warmth and light. In agricultural societies, winter was the most feared time of the year, a time when food was scarce and the cold could kill. It is no wonder that Marzanna became associated with death and decay, **her icy touch a harbinger of suffering**.

But **there is power in her coldness**, in the dormancy that winter demands. The earth cannot produce fruit without first lying fallow, and so too must we allow parts of ourselves to rest, to wither, so that new life can take root. **Marzanna teaches the wayfarer that death is not something to be feared**, but something to be understood as part of the natural order.

In ancient times, the Slavs would **honor Marzanna** at the end of winter, performing rituals to send her back to the underworld. **They would make a doll from straw**, dress her in rags, and parade her through the fields before burning or drowning her in a nearby river. This act was not just to rid themselves of winter's chill but to honor the cycle of death and rebirth, to acknowledge Marzanna's power and then send her away so that spring could arrive.

Marzanna's darker aspects are many. In some tales, she appears as **Mora**, the **personification of fate** and a malevolent spirit who torments men in the night. **She is a shapeshifter**, a tormentor who feeds off fear and suffocates her victims in their sleep. In these stories, **Mora represents the nightmares that haunt us**, the dark thoughts we try to avoid. But even in this form, she is not evil. **She is the shadow we all carry within**, the fear of change, of loss, of death. *And through facing her, we can find our strength.*

In another guise, **Marzanna becomes Marui**, the kitchen demon who hides behind stoves and plays tricks on those who forget to honor her. She **twirls like a shadow**, her presence felt in the smallest disturbances, reminding us that the domestic realm is also a place of power. Even here, **Marzanna's influence is felt** — in the heat of the oven, the transformation of raw ingredients into sustenance, the ever-present potential for creation and destruction.

As a **wayfarer seeking grounding**, Marzanna teaches you to embrace the darkness, the quiet of winter, and the stillness of death. She reminds you that **rebirth can only come through the acceptance of endings**. Her cycle of death and renewal is not just about the changing seasons but about the changes within you. **You must let parts of yourself die** — old fears, limiting beliefs, the things that no longer serve you — before you can be reborn.

Marzanna's mythology intertwines with the sun gods and the hunt, much like **Persephone and Demeter's tale**. When Marzanna seduces the Huntsman, the god of the sun, she traps his light in a magic mirror, **cutting the world off from warmth and light**. In her jealousy and grief, winter descends, and **the world plunges into darkness**. But each spring, her sister **Zhiva** returns, restoring balance and allowing the warmth of the sun to return.

In Marzanna's story, **you find the eternal dance of light and dark, life and death**. Her **icy grip may seem relentless**, but within it lies the promise of rebirth. As you walk your path, **she challenges you to face the darkness head-on**, to confront your own winter, and to trust that spring will come. **Her power lies not in the cold itself**, but in the understanding that from death comes life, from stillness comes movement, and from darkness comes light.

HİNDU GODDESSES

In the vast and intricate tapestry of Hindu mythology, there exists a profound and mysterious reverence for the **Dark Goddesses**. These goddesses—**Kali**, **Durga**, **Chinnamasta**, and **Chamunda**—carry with them not only the power of creation and destruction but the intense and raw energy of transformation. **As a wayfarer**, seeking inner grounding and clarity, you will find in them reflections of your own journey through the shadows, through the dark places of the soul where change is born.

Hindus understand the universe through the lens of Brahman, the supreme, all-encompassing divine energy. While Brahman represents the ultimate truth and reality, its myriad facets manifest in the form of **many gods and goddesses**. Each one embodies a different aspect of Brahman's characteristics, offering pathways for those who seek understanding and enlightenment. Among these deities, **the Dark Goddesses stand apart**—powerful, fierce, and sometimes terrifying. Yet, they are not simply to be feared. **They are guides for those who dare to explore the depths** of their own being, teaching that even in destruction, there is the potential for rebirth.

Kali, perhaps the most well-known of the Dark Goddesses, is both feared and revered for her formidable power. Clad in darkness, her skin as black as the void, she stands as the ultimate destroyer of illusion. **As a wayfarer**, when you encounter Kali, she strips away everything that is false, everything that holds you back from embracing your true nature. She demands truth and nothing less. **Her wild hair**, unbound and flowing, symbolizes the untamed forces of the universe, and her necklace of skulls reminds you that life and death are intertwined in an endless dance. *Kali teaches you that to truly know yourself, you must face the death of the ego, the destruction of the identities you cling to.*

But Kali is not simply a goddess of death; she is the **mother of time**, the one who brings forth the cycles of life. In her destructive aspect, she clears away the old, making way for the new. **She cradles her devotees in the fierce arms of transformation**, urging you to let go of your fears and embrace the unknown. **Her blood-soaked tongue**, often depicted in art, speaks to the rawness of her power—her ability to cut through the false layers of reality and reveal the primal truths that lie beneath. *For those seeking inner grounding, Kali's lesson is simple but difficult: surrender to the process of destruction, for only then can you be reborn.*

Durga, on the other hand, embodies the divine warrior, **the fierce protector of all that is just and righteous**. She rides into battle, her many arms wielding weapons of divine power, her eyes filled with unwavering focus. In her presence, you sense not the destruction of self, as with Kali, but the empowerment to defend your true self against all forces that seek to diminish it. **Durga stands for the inner strength you possess**, that quiet resolve within you that refuses to bow to external pressures. She represents the **divine feminine energy that will not be tamed or suppressed**, a reminder that even in the darkest of times, there is a warrior within you waiting to rise.

Durga's power is undeniable. She defeats the demons that threaten the cosmos, but more importantly, she defeats the **inner demons** that plague your heart and mind—doubt, fear, insecurity. *Her energy is the fire of self-empowerment*, burning away the limitations you place on yourself. As you search for grounding, **Durga whispers to you that sometimes the path**

forward requires battle—not with others, but with the parts of yourself that resist change.

Chinnamasta, another Dark Goddess, confronts you with a vision both shocking and deeply symbolic. She stands **headless**, holding her own severed head in one hand, while her blood flows freely, nourishing those around her. **Chinnamasta's symbolism is profound**—she represents the ultimate act of self-sacrifice, the surrender of the self for the greater good. **For the wayfarer**, she challenges you to let go of your attachment to the mind, to the ego's need for control. **Chinnamasta shows you that true power lies not in the self, but in the ability to transcend it**, to give of yourself freely, without expectation.

In her presence, **you are reminded of the beauty of letting go**, of allowing the divine energy to flow through you without clinging to form or identity. **Her severed head** symbolizes the need to release the overthinking mind, to quiet the constant chatter that keeps you from experiencing the fullness of the present moment. *Chinnamasta's fierce image teaches you that surrender is not weakness, but a form of ultimate strength*—the strength to trust in the process, even when it feels like you are losing everything.

Chamunda, the most fearsome of the Dark Goddesses, embodies the energy of death, destruction, and the fierce power of the feminine unleashed. **She is the devourer of demons**, and her image is often terrifying—sunken eyes, emaciated body, and a necklace of severed heads. Yet, within this fearsome exterior lies a profound truth. **Chamunda shows you that you cannot shy away from the darkness within**. You must face it head-on, unflinching, if you are to emerge stronger and more grounded.

Her energy is that of the **darkest night**, the place where all fears and insecurities are laid bare. **But in this darkness**, Chamunda reminds you that there is also power, **the power to destroy what no longer serves you**, to rid yourself of the limitations that hold you back. *Chamunda teaches that sometimes destruction is necessary, not as an act of cruelty, but as an act of liberation.* **When you face her**, you are forced to confront your deepest fears, but in doing so, you gain the power to overcome them.

Each of these **Dark Goddesses carries with her a unique energy**, a powerful force that both destroys and creates. **As a wayfarer**, you may be drawn to their mysteries because they resonate with something deep within you—the understanding that to find your true power, you must first confront the shadows within. **Kali**, **Durga**, **Chinnamasta**, and **Chamunda** are not just goddesses of destruction; they are **goddesses of transformation**, urging you to release what holds you back and embrace the fierce power that lies dormant within.

In their stories, you find your own—the struggle between light and dark, creation and destruction, death and rebirth. They guide you through these cycles, showing you that **grounding is not about holding on to stability, but about finding strength in the constant flow of change**. *In surrendering to the forces of transformation*, you become grounded in a deeper, more lasting way—**rooted not in the illusion of permanence, but in the ever-changing, ever-evolving nature of life itself**.

Kali

With her black or blue skin, tongue dripping with blood, and a necklace of skulls around her neck, she stands as a powerful figure. **Wayfarer**, you may feel a chill when you first encounter her image, for Kali embodies the destruction of illusion, the end of ego, and the power of transformation. Yet beneath her fierce exterior, there is a motherly force, one who nurtures and protects her devotees with a love as intense as her wrath.

In the ancient myths, Kali was born from the wrath of the war goddess **Durga**, who could no longer contain her fury while battling the buffalo demon, **Mahishasura**. As Durga struggled, her anger manifested into Kali, a being of pure destruction. Kali devoured the demons that plagued the world, wearing their heads like trophies in the form of a necklace. Her skirt, made of severed arms, is a stark reminder of her unstoppable power.

You, as a seeker of your own truth, may look at Kali with awe and fear, but you must understand that her violence is not without purpose. Kali's destruction is aimed only at the demons of ignorance, ego, and illusion. She doesn't destroy for pleasure, but to cleanse, to make space for something more profound. **In her mythology, Kali only attacks those who threaten the cosmic balance**, ensuring that truth and justice prevail.

Kali's story also shows us the depths of her ferocity, as there are times when even the gods tremble before her. Once, in her bloodlust, she could not stop her rampage. It wasn't until she stepped on her husband, **Shiva**, lying down in her path, that she was brought back to her senses. **In that moment**, Kali recognized that even she needed to pause, to find balance between destruction and creation. *This moment of recognition was not a* *defeat, but a reminder of the balance between the wildness within and the calm that must follow.*

In another telling of her birth, Kali arose when the gods needed a savior to defeat the demon **Daruka**, who could only be slain by a woman. Without hesitation, Kali answered the call, putting an end to his terror. And in the story of **Raktabija**, a demon whose every drop of blood created new demons, Kali's solution was simple: she devoured them all, ensuring that no blood could spill and multiply the threat.

But even in these fierce depictions, **Kali is not simply a goddess of war and violence**. She is, at her core, a mother figure, protecting those who seek her guidance and destroying only to rebuild. **Her love is as boundless as her power**, and she is often depicted in ancient poems as youthful, voluptuous, and irresistible, despite the terrifying imagery often associated with her.

As a wayfarer, you might feel drawn to Kali's power, feeling the pull of her fierce energy. But her lesson is clear: to find your truth, you must be willing to destroy the illusions that bind you. She holds both the sword of destruction and the hand of blessing, offering both fear and comfort, destruction and protection. **In this duality lies her true nature**, and it is through her that you can connect with your own inner strength, your own wildness, and the deep maternal love that guides you.

There is a common misconception about **Kali**, which is important to clarify. Kali is often mistakenly connected to the demon **Kali** of the Kali Yuga — the age of darkness and moral decline in Hindu cosmology. But these two are not the same. **Kali, the goddess**, stands for destruction that leads to rebirth, whereas **the demon Kali** represents chaos without creation, the end without renewal. Kali, the goddess, empowers you to face the darkness within, to conquer your fears, and to rise from the ashes stronger than before.

Kali is often revered in her many forms, each carrying a different facet of her immense power. Whether she is seen as **Dhumavati**, the widow who symbolizes loss and death, or **Bhairavi**, the fierce mother who embraces both life and destruction, **Kali's energy speaks to the cycles of life, death, and rebirth**. She reminds you that even in the darkest moments, there is the possibility of new life, new growth, and transformation.

In one story, a group of thieves kidnaps a monk and plans to kill him near a statue of Kali. The goddess, enraged by their intention to harm an innocent, brings the statue to life and destroys the thieves. Here, we see Kali not just as a destroyer, but as a protector of the righteous, one who punishes evil and upholds the balance of the universe.

In her nakedness, Kali embodies purity and freedom, stripped of all societal expectations and illusions. She represents sexuality, not in its tame, civilized form, but in its raw, untamed power. **She reminds you** that to be whole, to be grounded, you must embrace all parts of yourself—your darkness, your desires, your anger, and your love. There is no shame in her; there is only truth.

As you look to Kali for guidance, you may feel her energy awaken something deep within you. She does not shy away from the difficult truths, and neither should you. **Her gaze is direct, unflinching**, as she urges you to confront what you fear most about yourself. She asks you to step into the fire, knowing that though it may burn, it will also purify.

Wayfarer, in Kali's embrace, you will find a new kind of grounding. It is not the kind that comes from stillness or stability, but from a deep understanding that you can survive the destruction of your old self. **Kali asks you to let go** of what no longer serves you, to be unafraid of the darkness within, and to embrace the power that comes from transformation.

When you invoke Kali, you are calling on the very force of nature that destroys to create. **In your ritual, when you light the candle and call her name, you are asking for her to guide you through your own rebirth**, to help you cut through the illusions and attachments that keep you from your truth. And as you meditate on her image, let her fierce, protective energy fill you, reminding you that you are both warrior and nurturer, both destroyer and creator.

Durga

Durga stands as a force beyond comprehension—a warrior goddess born from the combined powers of the most supreme deities. **Wayfarer**, as you seek grounding, know that Durga is not merely a goddess to behold; she is an energy, a force, a protector who surrounds you when the world feels uncertain.

Her origins tell us much about her role in the vast tapestry of Hindu mythology. The world was in turmoil, gripped by fear as **Mahishasura**, the buffalo demon, wreaked havoc upon the earth and the heavens. Neither gods nor men could quell the terror he spread. In this moment of crisis, the Supreme Triad—**Shiva**, **Brahma**, and **Vishnu**—came together. Out of their combined energies, **Durga** emerged. She wasn't born as a child, tender and needing growth. No, she came forth fully formed, radiant, and fierce—**a warrior ready for battle**, a protector of all creation.

Her **eight arms**, each holding a weapon, were not just for the destruction of physical demons but the demons within—anger, arrogance, greed, and pride. In her battle with Mahishasura, she showed her relentless power, fighting him as he morphed into various forms. And when he finally took the shape of a buffalo, **Durga's blade cut through his illusion**, slaying him and restoring balance to the universe.

You, too, may feel a connection to this warrior goddess when life feels like a battlefield. Perhaps it's not demons like Mahishasura you face, but challenges that test your strength, your resolve, your boundaries. **Durga reminds you** that even in the face of overwhelming odds, you are never powerless. **Her energy is within you**, a reminder that you can fight back against the forces that try to diminish you, both within and without.

Her name, **Durga**, holds deep meaning. Derived from the Sanskrit word for "fort," it signifies her role as an unbreakable fortress—a guardian who shelters and protects those who seek her. She is also called **Durgatinashini**, which means "the one who eliminates all sufferings." **Wayfarer, think about that for a moment**—to eliminate all suffering. That is the essence of her energy. **When you feel overwhelmed**, remember that Durga fights not only for the external battles but for the inner battles you face. Her power is your power.

And yet, **Durga is not a goddess of mindless destruction**. There is grace, there is control, and above all, there is compassion. **She rides upon a lion**, her movements calculated, her energy balanced. The lion, a symbol of strength and control, reflects Durga's ability to tame the wildness within. Her weapons, while formidable, are tools of **transformation**, not simply of death. **The sword she holds is not just for cutting down enemies, but for cutting through ignorance, slicing through the illusions that cloud your path.**

In some stories, **Durga is also referred to as Tryambake**, the three-eyed goddess. Her **right eye** represents the sun, the force of action. Her **left eye** embodies the moon, the essence of desire and emotion. And her **middle eye**, the eye of fire, symbolizes pure knowledge. **In this way, she encompasses all aspects of existence**—from action to emotion to wisdom. **When you call upon her**, you are calling on the energy to see clearly through the chaos.

Durga's myth is rich in symbols, but none more potent than her victory over Mahishasura. This wasn't just a battle of physical force; it was a battle of energies. The demon represented the ego, the destructive qualities of the human mind. **Durga's victory symbolizes the triumph of consciousness over unconsciousness, of awareness over ignorance**. She fights so

that you can reclaim the clarity that lies within you, even when the world outside appears dark and tumultuous.

Her **duality** is what makes her such a powerful goddess for those on the path of inner discovery. She is both destroyer and nurturer, both fierce and compassionate. **Wayfarer, if you are seeking grounding**, you need both of these energies within yourself. You need the fire of destruction to burn away what no longer serves you, and you need the gentleness of compassion to nurture what is good and true in your life.

Durga's image, with her eight arms and weapons, might seem overwhelming at first glance. But look deeper, and you will see a balance—an understanding that power, when used with wisdom, can bring peace. Each of her weapons represents a different aspect of her divine nature: the sword for truth, the trident for healing, the lotus for purity. **She is always ready, always equipped to fight from all directions**. And so must you be, as you journey through life's trials, knowing that you, too, can defend yourself against the many forces that try to pull you away from your path.

One of Durga's most significant messages is about **boundaries**. **She teaches you to protect your energy**—to set limits with those who drain your strength. Her ability to fight on all fronts is a reminder that you, too, have the power to shield yourself from negativity, to protect your heart from those who would bring you harm. But she also teaches compassion—for she fights not out of malice, but to protect the world, to restore balance. **When you embody Durga's energy**, you can set boundaries without shutting people out. You can be strong without being hard. You can fight without losing your compassion.

Durga's energy is not just a concept. It is something you can feel, something you can call upon when you need it. In moments of doubt or fear, when the challenges of life seem too great, take a deep breath, and remember that Durga is with you. **She is the voice within you that says, "I will not give up."** She is the strength in your bones, the fire in your soul.

In invoking Durga's presence, **wayfarer, you are calling upon the deepest reserves of your own strength**. Her message is clear: fight for what is right, fight for what is true, but always from a place of inner peace. Let her be your guide, not just in moments of battle, but in moments of quiet strength, where your boundaries are firm, your heart is open, and your mind is clear.

Durga reminds you that you are powerful beyond measure, and with her energy, you can overcome any obstacle.

Chinnamasta

In the shadows of the cosmos, **Chinnamasta** stands as a goddess whose very form challenges the wayfarer to confront the complexities of life and death, of desire and self-control. **Her name — "the one with the severed head" — immediately evokes an image that is both unsettling and powerful**. And yet, as with all Dark Goddesses, what lies beneath the surface is a profound truth waiting to be revealed.

Wayfarer, as you seek your inner grounding, **Chinnamasta** calls you to look beyond the terrifying image and see the sacred act of self-sacrifice, of transformation, and the immense strength of the feminine force. She is not merely a symbol of severance but a guide to understanding the depths of surrender and empowerment that come when one lets go of the ego, the attachment, and the illusion of control.

One day, as the tale goes, **Parvati**, the goddess of love and fertility, wandered with her attendants to the sacred waters of the **Mandakini River**. There, something deep within her shifted — her body darkened, and an unfamiliar surge of energy coursed through her veins. Her attendants, too, were seized by an inexplicable hunger, their eyes pleading for nourishment. And in that moment, **Parvati**, driven by both **feminine compassion** and fierce love, made an extraordinary choice. She drew her sword and, in a swift motion, severed her own head, allowing streams of blood to flow from her neck, nourishing her attendants with the essence of life itself. It was an act of ultimate surrender, one that **defied the natural order** but spoke to a deeper truth about sacrifice and love.

Wayfarer, this myth is not just about Parvati or Chinnamasta. It is about **you**. It speaks to the times when you may feel overwhelmed by desire or burdened by those who look to you for guidance, for sustenance, for strength. And yet, like Chinnamasta, you find that the only way to truly give is to surrender a piece of yourself. But this severing — this act of letting go — does not destroy you. Instead, it reveals a deeper power within.

In another telling of her origin, **Chinnamasta** was born from the fierce battle between the gods and demons. When the gods could no longer withstand the might of their enemies, they turned to **Mahashakti**, the supreme goddess, for aid. She came forth with an unparalleled fury, slaying the demons without mercy. And yet, in her victory, she turned her sword upon herself, drinking her own blood as a reminder that power unchecked, even in the service of good, must be tempered by self-reflection and restraint.

This duality is at the heart of **Chinnamasta. She is both creator and destroyer, both nurturer and fierce warrior**. She embodies the **dark feminine energy** that many fear, but few understand. Her image — a naked, fierce goddess holding her severed head in one hand and a sword in the other — may seem unsettling at first. But look closer, **wayfarer**, and you will see that she represents the paradox of life itself. **In her nakedness, she sheds the trappings of the material world**. Her severed head, far from being a symbol of death, represents **the ultimate release from ego and attachment**. And in the streams of blood that flow from her neck, she gives life to those around her.

Chinnamasta stands over the dead, not as a goddess of destruction, but as one who has conquered her desires, her fears, and her limitations. She challenges you to do the same. To stand over the parts of yourself that no longer serve you, the fears and attachments that keep you from fully embracing your true power.

In the symbolism of **Chinnamasta**, every detail holds meaning. **The serpent around her neck** speaks of the primal power of transformation — shedding the old skin to reveal the new. Her severed head, drinking the blood from her own neck, shows that true empowerment comes from within. **She is not fed by external sources**, but by the deep well of strength that resides in her core. **Wayfarer, can you find that strength within yourself**? Can you sever the ties that bind you to old patterns and nourish yourself with the truth of who you really are?

Though she may seem terrifying, **Chinnamasta** is, at her core, a mother. **She sacrifices not out of rage, but out of love**. She does not take life meaninglessly — she gives life by severing her own head, symbolizing the **death of the ego**. In this, she teaches us that **sometimes, the most profound transformation comes from letting go** of what we think we need to hold onto most. Her story, like that of so many Dark Goddesses, asks you to look beyond the surface and to see the deeper truths hidden within.

Chinnamasta's fierce, naked form is a reminder that we must confront the rawest parts of ourselves, the parts we often try to hide. **She invites you to strip away the layers** of protection, of false identity, of the ego that tells you that you are separate from the divine. **Her sword is your tool to cut through these illusions**, to reveal the power that lies at the heart of your being.

To some, **Chinnamasta's act of severing her head** might seem like madness. But there is **a deeper wisdom** in her actions. **It is a reminder that to truly give, we must first release what no longer serves us**. Her courage, her sacrifice, and her willingness to confront the darkest parts of herself are gifts she offers to you. **Will you accept them**?

As you walk your path, **wayfarer**, let **Chinnamasta's** story be a guide. When you feel overwhelmed by the demands of life, when the weight of expectations presses down on you,

remember that you have the power to sever those ties. You have the strength to stand in your truth, even when it means confronting the darkest parts of yourself. And in doing so, you will find that **you are not diminished**, but made whole.

Chinnamasta is not a goddess of destruction for its own sake. She is a goddess of transformation, of letting go, of surrendering to the process of life and death, creation and destruction. She reminds us that **there is no creation without destruction**, no birth without death, no transformation without sacrifice. **And in her fierce love**, she shows us that the most profound gifts often come from the most painful places.

As you seek your own inner grounding, **Chinnamasta** encourages you to embrace both the light and the dark within you. To find the strength to let go of what no longer serves you, and to trust that in the surrender, **you will find your true power. Her severed head is not a symbol of loss, but of liberation**. And as you walk your path, **wayfarer**, may you find that same liberation within yourself.

Chamunda

Chamunda, a goddess born from blood, war, and fire—yet she is also a mother, a protector, and a force of transformation.

Before **Chamunda** became a part of the Hindu pantheon, she was already worshiped by different tribes. Her origins are shrouded in the mists of time, but one thing is clear: her power is ancient, her presence undeniable. Unlike many goddesses who are born into the light, **Chamunda** emerged from the darkness, forged in battle and fury. **Her existence** was a response to the rise of demons, and her purpose was clear—to restore balance through destruction, to protect through annihilation.

The story of **Chamunda** begins with two ambitious demon brothers, **Shumbha** and **Nishumbha**, who sought to conquer the world. They tortured themselves for thousands of years, hiding in a temple to gain the favor of **Brahma**, the creator god. When they impressed him with their acts of devotion, **Brahma** granted them a reward. The brothers chose immortality in a very specific form: no man, no male god could ever harm or kill them. And with this gift, they grew unstoppable, wreaking havoc upon the earth, pushing the gods into the shadows of fear.

The gods, powerless against the demons, turned to **Devi Parvati**, the supreme goddess. She watched and waited, knowing that she alone had the power to stop them. **Wayfarer, Chamunda's story is about patience and the stillness before the storm.** **Parvati** positioned herself near the demons, quietly, knowing they would notice her. And they did. Her beauty caught the eye of one of their attendants, who reported back to **Shumbha**. The demon was captivated by her and sent messengers to request her presence. But **Parvati** refused. The demons grew angry, suspicious that someone was backing her resistance. They ordered their army to force her submission. And it was then that **Chamunda** was born.

In a roar of defiance, **Chamunda** erupted from the forehead of **Devi Parvati**. The battlefield became her domain. She was a force of nature — her thick red hair framed a face of unrelenting power, her eyes blazed with the fire of battle. **Her skin, blood-red**, mirrored the blood she was about to spill. And with her arrival, the tide of battle turned. She devoured **Chanda** and **Munda**, two of the most feared generals of the demon army, **earning the name Chamunda** — a name etched in blood and victory.

As **Chamunda** danced in triumph, her energy pulsed through the earth, shaking even the gods. **Wayfarer**, there is a deep mystery in this dance of destruction.

To stand in the presence of **Chamunda** is to feel the paradox of her nature — **fierce and loving, terrifying and compassionate**. She is a goddess of war, famine, and disasters, yet she is also a mother figure, a protector of those who call upon her in need.

Her appearance alone evokes both awe and fear.

Three eyes, each burning with intensity, symbolize her all-seeing nature. She gazes not only at the external world but deep into your soul, uncovering what lies hidden in your heart.

Four arms, each holding a weapon, show her readiness to fight at any moment from any direction. She wears a necklace of skulls — each one a testament to her victories over the demons of the world. And yet, **beneath the skulls and weapons, there is a tenderness**. The blood she spills is not senseless; it is deliberate, a protective force meant to safeguard the cosmic order.

Chamunda, like many Dark Goddesses, walks the line between creation and destruction.

She does not kill out of rage, but out of necessity. The demons she slays are not merely enemies — they are manifestations of **arrogance, greed, and chaos**, the very forces that threaten harmony. **Wayfarer**, there is something for you to learn here. **Chamunda asks you to confront your own demons** — the thoughts, behaviors, and patterns that keep you bound. She stands as a reminder that true power lies in both the ability to create and the courage to destroy what no longer serves you.

Her connection to **Shiva** — the god of destruction — amplifies her energy. Together, they embody the duality of life and death, the balance of the universe. She is often invoked to remove obstacles, to bring justice, and to banish negative forces. But in doing so, she also demands that you **look within and see the shadows you need to release**.

Though she may appear fearsome, **Chamunda** is not an indiscriminate force of destruction. She responds to those who seek her with a pure heart, those who are willing to face their fears and their darkness.

She is a guide through the shadows, showing you that there is no need to fear the dark when you carry the light of your own strength within.

As you walk your path, **wayfarer**, know that **Chamunda** is there with you, her fierce energy protecting you from harm, but also pushing you to confront the truth of who you are.

She asks you to be brave enough to step into the unknown, to embrace the chaos and emerge from it transformed.

When you invoke her, do so with reverence.

Understand the depth of her power and the lessons she brings. She is not a goddess to be called lightly, but she is always willing to protect those who show her respect and devotion.

Wayfarer, as you journey further into yourself, trust that the strength of **Chamunda** flows through you.

 Her fierce love, her unwavering protection, and her ability to destroy what no longer serves you — **these are the gifts she offers**.

And when you are ready, she will guide you through the darkest parts of yourself, helping you to emerge, stronger and more aligned with your true power.

Hiḍimbā

the forests of ancient lore are filled with secrets, where gods and demons walk among mortals. In one such forest, amidst towering trees and shadows thick with mystery, a story unfolds — one that speaks of power, transformation, and love beyond the boundaries of the ordinary. This is the tale of **Hiḍimbaa**, the fierce **rakshasi** who crossed paths with **Bhīma**, the mighty warrior of the **Pāṇḍavas**. Her presence, both terrifying and enchanting, is a reminder that strength often emerges from unexpected places.

As the **Pāṇḍavas** sought refuge in the deep woods, escaping their enemies, they unknowingly stepped into **Hiḍimbaa's** domain. The night was thick, and while the others slept, **Bhīma** stood watch. There, beneath the dense canopy, another kind of watch was taking place. **Hiḍimbā**, **Hiḍimbaa's** brother, caught the scent of the **Pāṇḍavas** from afar. His bloodlust awakened, and he sent his sister to lure the strongest of them, **Bhīma**, into a trap so he could devour him.

But, **wayfarer**, not everything in this world follows a simple path. **Hiḍimbaa**, a **rakshasi**, a creature meant to incite fear and destruction, found herself stirred by something else entirely as she approached **Bhīma**. **Love bloomed where there should have only been hunger.** She was drawn not to his flesh, but to the power in his heart, the strength in his soul. Transformed, she appeared before him not as the terrifying figure she was, but as a woman of breathtaking beauty, her fierce spirit softened by the pull of love.

She revealed her truth to **Bhīma**, **wayfarer** — not hiding behind deceit, but standing in her raw honesty. **Hiḍimbaa** spoke of her brother's intentions, of the danger that awaited. But in her revelation, she also confessed her desire, a longing that defied the laws of her kind. Her honesty became her power, and with this, **Bhīma** understood the depth of her courage. **Hiḍimbā**, the fearsome rakshasa, soon met his match in **Bhīma**, who overpowered and defeated him in a battle that thundered through the forest. The fight wasn't just for survival—it was for the possibility of something more.

In the aftermath of the battle, **Hiḍimbaa** stood not as an enemy, but as an ally. Her love for **Bhīma** had shifted the course of her destiny. She asked to be his wife, to walk beside him despite the worlds that separated them. And so, they were married in that forest, **wayfarer**, under the canopy of ancient trees, the air still thick with the echo of battle. But this union was not meant to be a permanent one. **Bhīma**, bound by duty and destiny, promised to stay with her only until a child was born. **Hiḍimbaa**, in her love and wisdom, accepted this with grace.

In time, their son was born—a boy named **Ghaṭotkacha**, his head resembling a pot, a symbol of the unexpected and the extraordinary. This child, born of the earth and sky, would grow into a formidable warrior, his presence in the great **Mahābhārata** war a testament to the power that flowed from both his parents.

But, **wayfarer**, there is more to **Hiḍimbaa's** story than her union with **Bhīma**. After he left her to continue his journey, she remained in the forest, dedicating herself to a path of spiritual transformation. She was not just a wife, nor merely a mother— she was a goddess in her own right. **Hiḍimbaa**, once a fearsome rakshasi, entered a life of penance and prayer, her fierce energy redirected toward the divine. Her name became synonymous with strength, resilience, and transformation. Over time, she was worshipped, and temples rose in her honor, her legacy woven into the very fabric of the land.

In **Manali**, a temple stands, dedicated to **Hiḍimbaa**, the once-demon who became a goddess. It is a place of reverence, where the air is thick with the memory of her power. People come to honor her, to seek her blessings, not as a fearful demon but as a protector, a mother, and a guide. She is also worshipped in **Nepal**, at the **Bhutandevi Mandir**, where her fierce energy continues to be honored under the name **Bhuṭanadevī**, a goddess who guards and guides with her otherworldly wisdom.

Hiḍimbaa's tale, like the goddess herself, is layered with complexity, **wayfarer**. She is a being who walked between worlds—the mortal and the divine, the feared and the revered. Her strength came not just from her physical power, but from her ability to love fiercely, to fight for what mattered, and to transform her very nature. She teaches that within each of us lies the potential for transformation, that we are not bound by the roles we were born into. **Hiḍimbaa** stands as a reminder that we can choose our path, even when that path leads us through darkness and danger. And in doing so, we find our own power, our own light.

In the ancient forests of myth, where gods and demons roam, **Hiḍimbaa's** story whispers to those who seek it—those who are ready to embrace the strength within their own hearts, and who are willing to face the unknown with courage and love.

AFRICAN GODDESSES

Wayfarer, when you walk through the corridors of myth and legend, you will find that some paths are well-lit, while others remain cloaked in shadow. You've heard the stories of **Thor**, the thunderous god from the Norse realms, or **Aphrodite**, the radiant goddess of love from ancient Greece. Even **Cleopatra**, though not truly a goddess, is revered in Egyptian tales. But beyond these well-trodden roads, there lies another world, a realm not as frequently spoken of, yet rich in power and mystery — **ancient African mythology**.

In the heart of Africa, where the earth pulses with life and the air hums with spirits, there are goddesses as old as time itself. These are the Dark Goddesses — keepers of secrets, guardians of transformation, and embodiments of the primal forces of nature. Their names may not echo in the mainstream, but their power is undeniable. To walk in their world is to step into the shadows of creation, to touch the unseen energies that shape life and death.

One such goddess is **Oya**, the Yoruba goddess of storms, winds, and transformation. Her presence is felt in the howling winds before a storm, in the crackle of lightning that splits the sky, and in the shifting currents of change. **Oya** is not a goddess who offers gentle guidance. No, **wayfarer**, she sweeps through your life like a tempest, tearing down what no longer serves you, forcing you to confront the truth of who you are. To stand in her presence is to be caught in the eye of a storm, where the chaos of the world meets the stillness of your soul.

They say that **Oya** governs the winds that sweep across the earth, carrying with them the spirits of the dead. She is the gatekeeper of the afterlife, the one who guides souls through the veil and into the next realm. Her role is both feared and revered. She is the goddess who brings death, but also the one who brings rebirth. In her dark embrace, you find not only destruction but also the promise of renewal.

Another powerful figure is **Mami Wata**, the African goddess of the waters. She is as elusive as the depths of the oceans she commands, a goddess who embodies both beauty and danger. **Mami Wata** is often depicted as a mermaid, her body shimmering with scales, her gaze as hypnotic as the waves. She represents the depths of the subconscious, the hidden parts of the self that are as vast and mysterious as the sea. When she appears to you, it is a call to dive deep, to explore the uncharted waters of your soul, to confront the desires and fears that lie beneath the surface.

But be wary, **wayfarer**. **Mami Wata** is not to be taken lightly. She is a goddess who offers both blessings and curses. Her gifts are many — wealth, beauty, and love — but they come at a price. Those who invoke her must be prepared to face their innermost longings and to pay the cost of their desires. She does not grant her blessings freely, and her presence, like the sea, is both captivating and dangerous.

Then there is **Nzinga Mbande**, often seen not as a goddess in the traditional sense, but as a **warrior queen** whose legacy has transcended time, transforming her into a symbol of the fierce feminine spirit. Ruler of the **Ndongo and Matamba kingdoms**, **Nzinga** defied the Portuguese colonizers, leading her people with cunning, strength, and an unmatched willpower. Her story is not one of a mythical deity but a living force — an embodiment of resistance, resilience, and the dark, unyielding power that women possess when they are called upon to protect what they love.

As you read the tales of these goddesses, remember, **wayfarer**, that their darkness is not something to be feared. It is in the dark where transformation begins. The womb of the earth is dark, and from it springs life. The night is dark, but it is under its cover that stars shine the brightest. These African Dark Goddesses are not here to harm you; they are here to challenge you, to push you beyond your limits, to tear away the illusions that blind you from your true power.

These goddesses, like **Oya**, **Mami Wata**, and **Nzinga**, reflect a side of the divine feminine that is raw, unapologetic, and fiercely protective. They do not fit into the neat boxes of love, beauty, and fertility that other goddesses are often confined to. Instead, they remind you that power is not always gentle, that the feminine is not always soft. Sometimes, it is a storm, a tidal wave, a battle cry that echoes through the ages.

So as you walk this path, **wayfarer**, do not fear the shadows. Embrace them. For in the embrace of the Dark Goddesses, you will find not only the power to transform your life but the strength to stand in your own truth. These goddesses are not distant figures in the sky; they are within you, waiting to be awakened. **Their power is your power**—a force that can break chains, shatter illusions, and guide you through the darkest nights of your soul.

In their myths, you will find pieces of yourself. In their stories, you will discover the strength to claim your own power. These goddesses are not mere relics of the past; they are living forces that dwell in the heart of every woman who dares to face her darkness and emerge stronger for it. And as you learn their names, their symbols, their mysteries, you too will find the power to unveil the secrets of your own inner goddess.

Oya

Oya, a force both feared and revered, an **Orisha** of the Yoruba tradition. Unlike the deities you may know, Oya is not merely a goddess but a fierce intermediary between the living and the dead. She stands where the veil is thinnest, guiding the souls of the departed and watching over the graveyards.

Oya is the tempest. She can be the gentle breeze that caresses your skin or the howling storm that tears through your world, dismantling everything in its path. But her nature is not simply to destroy. She is also the Orisha of rebirth, of change, and of life beyond death. She exists where cycles begin and end—where transformation takes hold.

Her origins trace back to the heart of the Yoruba religion, and her name, **"O Ya"**, means "she tore." This is not just a name; it is a reflection of her very essence. She tears through the fabric of your life, shaking loose all that needs to fall away. She is the force of upheaval, the bringer of change, whether you are ready for it or not.

Wayfarer, as you journey through life, know that Oya is both protector and challenger. Her winds will strip away what no longer serves you, whether that be people, situations, or even your own illusions. She is the mother of transformation, urging you to release the old and make space for the new.

In **Yoruba mythology**, Oya was once human—a warrior, fierce and just, who liberated the enslaved and protected the weak. Her life was extraordinary, so much so that when she passed, she was gifted with an eternal role as an Orisha. She became a guardian of the dead, a fierce protector of women, and a force of nature. Her power is not one of quiet submission; it is the power of the storm.

Oya was married to **Shango**, the Orisha of thunder, a union as tumultuous as the forces they commanded. Together, they ruled over storms and lightning, their love a tempest as fierce as the weather they controlled. Oya, though favored by Shango, bore great sorrow, for none of her nine children survived birth. And so, she wears nine scarves, one for each child, keeping their memory alive even as she continues to rule over the winds and the dead.

But Oya is not a goddess to be pitied. Her grief has forged her into something stronger. She wields a **sword**, cutting through deceit and obstacles, bringing justice where it is needed. In her other hand, she carries a **fan**, able to stir the winds into storms, calling forth the forces of nature with the flick of her wrist.

Her domain stretches far and wide. She is the **Orisha of transformation**, destruction, and rebirth. She rules over **earthquakes**, **storms**, and **lightning**, guiding the elements themselves. She is also the keeper of the marketplace, where human desires collide with divine forces. It is said that those who lie or deceive in their dealings feel her wrath most acutely.

Oya also stands at the threshold of the afterlife. She is the guardian of the cemetery, watching over the spirits of the dead and ensuring that the balance between the living and the dead is maintained. When a soul is ready to pass, it is **Oya** who guides them to the other side, ensuring their safe passage. Yet, she also has the power to hold spirits back if their business in the world of the living is unfinished.

To call on Oya is to invite change into your life. Her energy is not gentle, but it is necessary. If you find your life stagnant, if the winds of transformation have stopped blowing, she may be the force you need. But be warned, **wayfarer**: Oya does not tolerate deceit, laziness, or injustice. If you seek her help, you must be prepared for the storm that follows. She will tear down what is weak and false, leaving only what is true and strong in its place.

Oya is also known as the **Great Mother of Witches**, the one who holds sway over the magic of life and death. She is a force of nature, and her power lies in her ability to traverse the realms of the living and the dead with ease. She is the ultimate guide for those who wish to communicate with their ancestors, to seek wisdom from beyond the grave, or to transform their lives entirely.

Wayfarer, if you feel Oya calling you, she will send signs. You may find yourself drawn to her symbols — **winds, storms, lightning** — or you may feel a sudden, unexplainable pull toward transformation. She may come to you in dreams, guiding you through upheaval, or you may feel her presence in the changes that sweep through your life, sudden and unbidden.

When the winds of change begin to blow, it is Oya who is behind them. Her lessons are not always easy, but they are always necessary. She teaches you to embrace the chaos, to find your strength in the storm, and to rise from the wreckage with a new sense of purpose. Her presence in your life signifies that you are ready for transformation, for rebirth, for the next chapter of your journey.

Should you wish to honor her, **wayfarer**, you can offer her things that resonate with her energy. **Plums, dark chocolate, red wine, or offerings of amber and moonstone** can be placed at her altar. But more than these material offerings, Oya values truth, justice, and the willingness to embrace change.

In the end, Oya is not just the goddess of storms and winds. She is the goddess of **life** and **death**, of **transformation** and **rebirth**. She holds the keys to the mysteries of existence, guiding you through the cycles of creation and destruction. To walk with her is to walk the path of **courage** and **transformation**. She is the storm that will clear the way for something new, something truer, to take root in your life.

And so, **wayfarer**, when you feel the winds begin to rise, know that **Oya** is near. Trust in her power, and let her guide you through the storm. For on the other side, you will emerge stronger, wiser, and more fully aligned with your true self.

Yewa

Wayfarer, you walk a path lined with mystery and shadow. As you seek the wisdom of the Dark Goddesses, you will find yourself standing at the edges of worlds, where life and death intertwine, where the living walk alongside the dead. One of the most enigmatic Orishas awaits you there — **Yewa**. She is Oya's sister, and like her, she rules over the cemeteries and the dead. Yewa is a figure shrouded in stillness and silence, guarding the boundaries of the graveyards, preventing the restless spirits from wandering among the living. She does not cause death, but she is the one who helps the souls find their final resting place. She is a guide, an escort, and a keeper of the sacred threshold.

Yewa's origins trace back to the **Yoruba religion**, her name meaning "Our Mother," derived from the words *Yeye* (mother) and *Awa* (our). She once stood as a protector of women and mothers, a powerful figure of fertility and water. Yet her story changed over time, and now she reigns as the Orisha of death, loneliness, and purity.

Wayfarer, Yewa was not always the dark and reclusive Orisha you see now. Once, she was a radiant beauty, a virgin known for her chastity. Many male Orishas desired her, their eyes drawn to her grace. Among them was **Shango**, a notorious womanizer who had seduced many female Orishas before. He pursued Yewa with a passion she could not resist, and though she fell for his charms, Shango abandoned her after she became pregnant, leaving her alone and shamed. Yewa's heart broke, her child lost, and she buried her pain along with the unborn baby beneath a tree. From that moment, she retreated into the shadows, living among the graves with her sister Oya, surrounded by the dead.

The myth of Yewa takes many forms. In one telling, **Olokun**, the Orisha of the depths, heard of her sorrow and, in his compassion, brought her lost child back to life. This child, **Borosia**, became Olokun's protector. Yet, Yewa remained in her graveyard realm, her beauty and purity tainted by the heartbreak she had endured.

In another version of her story, **wayfarer**, Yewa vowed never to fall again. She hid herself away, taking a vow of chastity and retreating to her father **Obatala**'s castle. But even there, her beauty was her curse. Word of her loveliness reached Shango once more, and he sought her out. This time, however, she was wiser. Torn between her desire and her fear of repeating the past, Yewa went to Obatala, seeking guidance. Her father, knowing her torment, sent her to the realm of the dead, where no living being could tempt her again.

Yewa now walks between worlds, the guardian of the dead, the protector of virgins, and the keeper of secrets. She is a figure of deep, mysterious power, with the ability to see beyond the veil of the living. Her connection to the spirits gives her wisdom beyond measure, and her clairvoyance is unmatched. She sees what others cannot, moving between life and death with the grace of one who has known both intimately.

Yewa is often depicted as a beautiful, slender woman dressed in pink, a color symbolizing both innocence and death. She is sometimes shown as an owl, flying silently through the night, her watchful eyes keeping vigil over the dead. Her demeanor is calm and wise, but there is no mistaking the depth of her power. **Wayfarer**, should you ever find yourself disrespecting her domain—mocking the dead, desecrating graves—you will feel the full force of her wrath. She is the guardian of the boundaries, and those who cross them without reverence will be reminded of their place.

Despite her somber role, Yewa is not a goddess of fear. She is a mother figure, a protector of the innocent, the pure, and the chaste. Her strength lies in her quiet resolve and her commitment to preserving the sanctity of life and death. She is the one who ensures that the dead remain at peace, dancing over their graves to soothe their restless souls.

If you feel called by Yewa, you may notice a pull toward solitude and introspection. You may find yourself drawn to the quiet places of the world—cemeteries, still waters, or even the silence within your own mind. Yewa's presence is often subtle, like the faint rustling of leaves in the wind, or the soft hoot of an owl in the distance. She comes to those who seek to understand the mysteries of life and death, those who wish to protect the sacredness of both.

To honor Yewa, **wayfarer**, approach her with reverence and respect. Never speak lightly of death or make crass jokes in her presence. Offer her **flowers, fish, or white hen meat**, but most of all, offer her your sincerity. Yewa does not tolerate deceit, nor does she take lightly the responsibility of her role. She will guide you if you are honest in your intentions, but she will not abide disrespect.

Yewa's story is one of transformation. From a naive and innocent virgin, she became a guardian of the dead, a protector of sacred boundaries, and a figure of immense power. She teaches us that even in the darkest places, there is purpose and strength. She shows us that loneliness can lead to wisdom, that heartbreak can forge resilience, and that death, like life, must be honored with respect and care.

Wayfarer, if Yewa calls to you, heed her voice. She may guide you through your own transformations, helping you navigate the changes and losses that life brings. She may offer you the gift of clarity, helping you see beyond the surface of things to the deeper truths that lie beneath. And in her silent, watchful way, she will remind you that even in the quietest moments, there is power.

Yewa stands at the threshold of life and death, watching, waiting, and protecting. She is the unseen force that ensures the balance between the realms, and if you are brave enough to walk with her, she may just show you the path to your own inner strength.

IRISH AND CELTIC GODDESSES

Wayfarer, as you journey deeper into the mists of ancient myth, you will encounter tales woven from the very fabric of mystery. The stories that have echoed across time — through whispered words by fireside and carried on the breath of the wind — now find their way to you. **Celtic** and **Irish Mythology** are not the same, though they share roots deep in the earth. Like branches from the same ancient tree, they have grown in different directions, yet each carries the power of an age-old world where gods, goddesses, and otherworldly beings walked among mortals. Irish mythology is, in fact, a rich offshoot of **Celtic beliefs**, preserved over centuries by the careful hands of Christian monks. These monks, while seeking to record history, also captured the essence of the old ways, ensuring that the tales of gods and goddesses, of magic and mystery, would not be lost to time. While the Irish branch may be the best preserved, its core is deeply intertwined with the broader Celtic mythology, home to stories of the **Scots** and **Brittonics**, tales of heroes, gods, and the powerful forces of nature that guided the lives of those who walked the land.

In the world of these mythologies, the gods and goddesses were not confined to simple, singular roles. Their dominions stretched across realms, touching every aspect of life — from love to fertility, from land to death. They did not stand alone, for the power of the divine was often shared, creating a web of influence that made it difficult to distinguish the exact boundaries of their dominion. The gods were vast and complex, just as the forces of nature that they commanded.

And so, as you step into this chapter, **wayfarer**, you are stepping into a place where the veil between worlds is thin. The air hums with the presence of gods and goddesses — dark and powerful figures, whose names inspired both reverence and fear in the hearts of the ancient Celts and Irish. The land itself seems alive with their memory, the hills and rivers whispering their stories.

In the **Celtic and Irish pantheon**, there is no shortage of mystery. These deities, many of them connected to the land, to the forces of nature, and to the otherworld, held a sway that was impossible to ignore. They were protectors, but they were also fierce. They could bring blessings, but they could just as easily bring curses. The line between life and death, between protection and destruction, was thin, and these deities stood at that threshold.

There is **Morrigan**, the goddess who embodies war, fate, and death. She is not one goddess, but many. A shape-shifter, a force of transformation, Morrigan is often depicted as a crow flying over battlefields, watching as the fates of men are sealed. She is a goddess of prophecy, foretelling the end of empires and the death of kings. To call on her is to invoke the very essence of death itself, to walk the fine line between life and the otherworld.

And there is **Brigid**, a goddess of fire and fertility, who holds both the warmth of life and the destructive force of flame in her hands. She is the protector of blacksmiths and poets, of those who work with both the tangible and the intangible. She is the healer and the destroyer, for her fire can warm and it can also burn.

The **Tuatha Dé Danann**, the ancient race of gods who once ruled Ireland, are ever-present in these stories. They are both divine and deeply tied to the land. They dwell in the **Otherworld**, a place of eternal youth and beauty, but they can also walk among mortals. Their powers are vast, and their influence stretches across the fields, forests, and rivers of Ireland. They are not always kind, but they are always just, and their presence is felt in every corner of the land. **Wayfarer**, as you read these tales, let yourself be drawn into the shadows of the ancient world. Feel the pulse of the earth beneath your feet, the murmur of the wind in your ear, and know that these stories are not simply myth—they are the very breath of the past, alive and waiting for those brave enough to listen. In this place, where gods and goddesses walk with mortals, you will find that the world is never as it seems. Every shadow holds a secret, every twist in the path a new revelation. The Dark Goddesses of **Celtic** and **Irish** mythology do not simply watch over the dead—they guide the living, as well, helping them to face their own inner darkness, to find strength in the most unexpected places.

And so, **wayfarer**, as you continue through this chapter, let the tales of these ancient deities inspire you. Feel the power of their stories, the weight of their presence, and allow yourself to walk the path between worlds, where the Dark Goddesses await. These are the goddesses who hold dominion over life and death, who remind us that there is power in both the light and the shadow, and that to truly know ourselves, we must face the darkness within.

This is the world of **Celtic** and **Irish myth**, where the lines between god and mortal, between life and death, are blurred. It is a world rich with magic, a world where every story is a lesson, every myth a mirror for the soul. Step into the shadows, **wayfarer**, and find the wisdom that waits there.

Morrigan

Wayfarer, you stand at the edge of a world where shadows dance with the light, where legends weave through the mist, and where the **Morrigan**, the Phantom Queen, awaits those brave enough to enter her realm. She is not simply a goddess — she is a force of nature, untamable and fierce, with power that both terrifies and fascinates.

In Celtic history, there is no figure as prominent or as enigmatic as the **Morrigan**. She stands alone, a formidable warrior, feared and worshiped in equal measure. She is a goddess of war, death, and fate, a shapeshifter who moves through the world in many forms. At times, she is a raven, her dark wings beating against the sky as she watches over battlefields, foretelling death. At others, she appears as a wolf, an eel, or even a beautiful woman — her beauty seductive, her intentions deadly.

But her most common form is that of a raven, a creature that has long been associated with death and the unknown. The raven, with its sharp beak and dark eyes, is a symbol of witchcraft and magic, both feared and revered. When the **Morrigan** takes this form, she brings with her the knowledge of what is to come — of battles lost and lives ended. Her presence on the battlefield is a prophecy in itself.

The **Morrigan**'s name carries its own power, as ambiguous and shifting as the goddess herself. Some say "Mor" comes from the old Irish word for phantom, while others link it to the Anglo-Saxon "maere," meaning nightmare. Whether she is the **Phantom Queen** or simply the **Great Queen**, her name alone is enough to send a shiver down the spine. And yet, **wayfarer**, she is more than just a goddess of war — she is a symbol of transformation, of the cycles of life and death, of destruction and rebirth.

In the stories passed down through generations, the **Morrigan** is sometimes portrayed as a single goddess, but often, she is part of a **triple goddess**, embodying the power of three: herself, **Macha**, and **Badb** (or **Neman**). Together, they form a triad of war goddesses, each representing a different aspect of battle, life, and sovereignty. To call upon the **Morrigan** is to invoke not just one powerful goddess, but the collective force of all three.

Her connection to war is undeniable, but she is also deeply tied to fertility and the land. She is both the **goddess of death** and the **guardian of life**, ensuring that the cycle of birth and death continues unbroken. Just as she can bring death, so too can she bring life and abundance, but only after the necessary destruction has taken place. She is, in many ways, a goddess of balance, ensuring that the world remains in harmony, even when that means bringing chaos.

Her power is not just limited to myth—she has inspired fear and reverence for centuries. **Wayfarer**, if you listen carefully, you might still hear the **Morrigan's** wings beating in the distance, or catch a glimpse of her shadow as it moves through the twilight. She is the very embodiment of transformation, and in her, you may find the courage to face your own inner battles.

One of the most famous tales of the **Morrigan** involves her encounter with the hero **Cu Chulainn**, a warrior whose fate was inextricably linked with the goddess. Their meeting was as much a battle of wills as it was a clash of physical force. **Cu Chulainn**, in his arrogance, did not recognize the **Morrigan** when he first met her. She appeared to him not as a goddess, but as a raven, and he insulted her, unaware of the power he had just slighted.

In retaliation, the **Morrigan** warned him of his impending death in battle, and true to her word, she appeared to him again before his final fight. Disguised as a beautiful woman, she offered him her love and protection, but **Cu Chulainn** refused, not knowing that he was turning away the goddess herself. In her rage, she transformed into an eel, a wolf, and then a cow, each time attempting to bring about his downfall. But **Cu Chulainn** was strong, and he fought back, injuring her in each form.

The goddess, though, was not easily defeated. She reappeared to him later, this time as an old woman, and through her trickery, **Cu Chulainn** unknowingly healed her wounds.

In their final encounter, just before his death, the **Morrigan** appeared to him as a raven, perching on his shoulder as he stood fast in battle, tied to a boulder, determined to die standing. In that moment, she claimed him, just as she had foretold.

The **Morrigan** is not a goddess to be trifled with. She does not forgive easily, nor does she forget. She is as relentless as the tides and as fierce as the storm, but she is also a protector, a guide for those who walk the path of the warrior.

Her presence in battle is both a blessing and a curse, for while she may foretell death, she also brings strength to those who are willing to fight.

Wayfarer, as you move through your own battles in life, remember that the **Morrigan** is always near. She is a goddess of transformation, of endings and beginnings, and in her, you may find the strength to face whatever challenges lie ahead. She teaches that from destruction comes rebirth, and from death, new life. To invoke her is to embrace your own power, to stand firm in the face of adversity, and to know that even in the darkest moments, there is always the possibility of renewal.

This is the power of the **Morrigan**, the Phantom Queen. She is
not just a figure of myth—she is the embodiment of the wild,
untamed forces that drive us all.

She is the goddess who stands at the threshold between life and
death, between light and darkness, and she invites you to walk
with her, to face your own shadows, and to emerge stronger on
the other side.

Macha

Wayfarer, let me tell you of **Macha**, a goddess whose name echoes through the fields of Ireland like a haunting whisper in the wind. She is a being of fierce power, a force to be reckoned with, yet deeply rooted in the land she protected. Her spirit is wild, untamed, and deeply connected to both the earth and the inevitable cycles of life and death. Like her sister, the **Morrigan**, Macha's stories are many, her forms shifting with the telling. But no matter which tale you follow, one truth remains — Macha is a goddess not to be forgotten.

In some myths, Macha is said to be part of the **Morrigan's** triad, but she also stands alone as a formidable member of the **Tuatha Dé Danann**, a powerful race of gods and goddesses who once ruled Ireland. She is **the goddess of kinship, fire, fertility, land, horses, and warfare**. Her magic was legendary, as was her unquenchable thirst for vengeance. Some say she lived in the ancient fort of **Emain Macha**, a place that still bears her name. It is a land that pulses with her memory, where every blade of grass carries whispers of her power.

Macha was not just a goddess of war, but of fertility as well — a duality that speaks to her complexity. She could bring life to the land, make it fertile and full, but she was also a death omen, an apparition who could foretell doom. As much as she nurtured, she destroyed, embodying the inevitable balance between creation and destruction. Her power was vast, her influence undeniable.

She was often associated with crows, horses, and the earth itself. These symbols of Macha remind us of her intimate connection to the land and the wild things that roam it. Her name, translating to "field" or "plain," suggests that she is woven into the very landscape of Ireland, as much a part of the soil as the roots of an ancient oak. **Wayfarer**, you can feel her presence in the quiet moments before a storm, in the stillness of the fields as the wind whispers through the grass, carrying with it both life and death.

The tales of **Macha** are many, but five stand out, each revealing a different facet of this complex goddess.

In one story, she is known as **Partholon's Daughter**, a figure from the **Leabhar Gabhala**, the Book of Invasions, which recounts how different groups of settlers came to Ireland. The **Patholonians**, some believe, were descendants of Noah, though they were wiped out by plague. Macha's mention in this tale is brief, but even here, her presence is unmistakable—she is the goddess of the land, tied to its cycles of life and death.

In another tale, Macha is part of the **Tuatha Dé Danann**, standing alongside her sister goddesses in the great battle of Moytura. Here, she is the goddess of war, conjuring rain, fog, blood, and fire to defeat her enemies. In this version of the story, Macha falls in battle, slain by the malevolent **Balor of the Baleful Eye**. Yet even in death, her legacy endures.

There is also the story of **Macha, the Wife of Nemed**, who arrived with the third wave of settlers to Ireland. This Macha, the goddess of fertility and land, dies while clearing the fields for planting, her body becoming one with the earth she loved. It is said that her grave lies in **Ard Mhacha**, the place known today as **Armagh**, further cementing her connection to the land.

Then there is the tale of **Macha, the Wife of Cruinniuc**, perhaps her most well-known story, found in the **Ulster Cycle**. In this version, Macha is a fairy woman, married to a wealthy farmer. She bore him twins and warned him never to speak of her to anyone. Yet, during a festival, Cruinniuc, in a moment of pride, boasted that his wife could outrun the king's horses. Furious, the king demanded Macha be brought to race, despite the fact that she was in labor. Macha won the race but collapsed in agony, giving birth at the finish line. In her pain and fury, she cursed the men of Ulster, condemning them to suffer the pains of childbirth for nine days during their greatest need. It was a curse that would last for nine generations, echoing through the ages.

Finally, there is the tale of **Macha of the Red Hair**. In this story, Macha is the daughter of **King Aodh Ruadh**. After her father's death, she claimed her right to rule in his place, challenging the two other kings who sought to deny her sovereignty because she was a woman. Macha was not easily defeated, and after killing one of her rivals, she reigned for seven years. She continued to prove her strength, even capturing her enemies by seduction and cunning. She forced them to build the fort of **Emain Macha**, a symbol of her unyielding power. Macha ruled alone for fourteen more years after her husband's death, until she herself was killed by **Rechtaid Rigderg**.

Each of these stories reveals the many faces of Macha: the goddess of fertility, the goddess of war, the goddess of vengeance. She is a protector, a destroyer, a mother, and a warrior. She is deeply tied to the land of Ireland, and her power is felt in every corner of it. To invoke **Macha** is to call upon the strength of the earth itself, to ask for her protection and her ferocity, to embrace the cycles of life and death.

Wayfarer, as you walk the path of your own life, remember that Macha is always near. Her spirit is in the wind that stirs the fields, in the cry of the raven as it circles the sky. She reminds us that we are part of something greater than ourselves — that we are bound to the land, to each other, and to the endless cycle of creation and destruction.

Badb

Wayfarer, let me lead you into the shadowed world of **Badb**, a goddess whose presence was both feared and revered by the ancient Celts. She is a dark figure, veiled in mystery, walking between life and death with the power to transform the tides of battle and fate. As one of the goddesses believed to complete the triad of the **Morrigan**, Badb is often seen as the manifestation of war itself, guiding the souls of the fallen and stirring the winds of chaos. Her name, steeped in ancient power, carries the weight of transformation and the inevitability of death.

They called her the **Battle Crow**, a name that spread fear across the battlefield. Wherever her black wings flew, **death was sure to follow**. Her keen eyes sought the spirits of the slain, and it was she who gathered them, leading them into the afterlife, where the next stage of their journey began. There was no escaping her, for she could see into the depths of each soul, knowing when it was time to move beyond this world. To face **Badb** was to stand at the edge of life and death itself.

Her presence was not subtle. Badb did not appear as a gentle guide but as a **petrifying woman**, draped in fear and chaos. She did not merely watch the battles unfold—she **wove the very fabric of war**, creating confusion and terror with each step. She was **war, transformation, and death**, embodying the awe that mortals felt when faced with forces beyond their control.

In her most terrifying form, **Badb** appeared as an old woman, her hair stark white, her clothes blood-red—a clear symbol of death in Celtic folklore. Her body was twisted into unnatural postures, with one foot lifted and one eye closed, representing the thin veil between life and the hereafter. As if drawn from the depths of the otherworld, she was not to be trifled with. And yet, there was wisdom in her ancient form, for she carried the power of **transformation**, offering something beyond death.

The **crow** and the **wolf** were her chosen symbols, creatures of darkness and transformation. When Badb flew over the battlefield as a crow, her appearance foretold death. She would swoop low over the soldiers, her black wings casting shadows on the ground as her fierce cries rang out, announcing the end of life. Her wolf, ever at her side, symbolized the raw hunger for battle and the cyclical nature of existence — life devouring life in the endless dance of survival.

But **Badb** was not just a goddess of death. Her story holds a deeper power, one tied to **rebirth** and **transformation**. There is an ancient tale of the **Cauldron of Rebirth**, a magical vessel that she stirred in the otherworld. When a warrior died in battle, their soul would be drawn to her, finding her standing by this cauldron. Her form, in that moment, might shift — no longer the terrifying figure of death but an old, kind woman, wise beyond measure. She would ask the fallen warrior a question that only the dead could answer: **"Will you remain or will you return?"**

Those who chose to be reborn were required to climb into the cauldron. As Badb stirred the water within, she would peer into its depths to divine their future. What form would they take? Would they return as human, or perhaps as an animal, free and wild? Her cauldron was the doorway to **transformation**, a reminder that from death springs new life.

Her power was not limited to the battlefield alone. In the **Battle of Magh Tuired**, Badb showed her might in all its glory. She appeared alongside her sisters, the Morrigan and Macha, as a **crow of terror**, filling the hearts of their enemies with dread. Together, their fierce voices echoed across the battlefield, speaking prophecies of **doom and defeat**. Her screams were the sound of **inevitable destruction**, and no warrior who heard her cries could escape the truth of their fate. The enemy armies were driven back into the sea, unable to withstand the weight of her presence.

And yet, after the battle was won, **Badb** did not simply disappear. She lingered, watching over families, her voice no longer one of war but of **warning**. She became the **banshee**, the wailing woman whose cry could be heard echoing through the night, signaling the death of a family member. Her role, though grim, was one of **protection** — for to hear her cry was to know that the time of death was near, and there was nothing more sacred than being prepared for that moment.

Wayfarer, if you find yourself drawn to Badb, know that she does not call to the faint of heart. She is a goddess of **war, transformation, and prophecy**, and her lessons are not easily learned. But if you walk with her, she will show you the power that lies in embracing both the light and the dark. She will teach you that death is not the end, but a part of the eternal cycle, a doorway to something more. You may hear her in the cry of a crow or feel her presence in the shifting winds of a storm. When you do, remember that she is both the end and the beginning, the one who guides us through the darkest places into the light.

Cailleach

Cailleach awaits you, her presence felt in the whispering winds of winter, in the biting cold that seeps into your bones. She is not a goddess of war, like Morrigan, but her power is no less fearsome. As the bringer of winter, she is the force that heralds the death of the year, the stillness before rebirth. Her name, **Cailleach**, means "the veiled one" — a fitting title for a goddess whose mysteries are shrouded in the mists of time, her face hidden beneath the cloak of winter's chill.

Her legend stretches beyond the borders of Ireland, reaching into the rugged landscapes of **Scotland** and the **Isle of Man**. There, too, she is known as the **goddess of the cold and wind**, her power felt in every fierce gust and biting frost. Those who speak of her tell tales of a **veiled old hag**, her skin pale and blue like the winter sky, her teeth stained red as though she has bitten into the very heart of life itself. She wears the marks of death — her clothes adorned with skulls, her presence a reminder that all things must wither in her cold embrace.

But the **Cailleach** is more than just the harbinger of winter. She is a **creator**, a force that shapes the land itself. In her hands, she wields a **hammer** that controls thunder and storms, much like the Norse god Thor. Some say she could leap across mountains, while others believe she could ride the winds of a storm as easily as a mortal walks the earth. Her shapeshifting powers allowed her to take the form of a **giant bird**, a dark omen in the sky, signaling the arrival of winter's grip.

Yet there is another side to **Cailleach**. She is not solely a bringer of death and destruction. In her mythology, she is deeply tied to the **cycle of life, fertility, death, and rebirth**. She is, after all, the one who brings the winter, but also the one who ushers it away.

When winter fades, so does she, allowing the land to come to life again. There is a strange beauty in this—**Cailleach** both withers and renews the world. She holds the balance between life and death, ensuring that neither overpowers the other.

In the telling of her stories, it's hard to say whether she is good or evil. Some see her as a cold, uncaring force, while others view her as a necessary part of the natural order. She is both feared and respected. Her love for animals, especially **wolves**, reveals a tenderness beneath the surface, though it is a wild, untamable love, like the wind itself.

One tale speaks of a wandering friar who encountered the **Cailleach** in her home, curious about her age. She told him that she did not know how long she had been alive, but each year, she would slaughter an ox and use its bones to make soup. If the friar truly wanted to know her age, she invited him to count the bones in her attic. The friar sent his scribe to the attic, and as the bones were tossed down, they began to pile up. The friar soon realized that his paper had run out, yet the bones kept coming. The scribe hadn't even cleared one corner of the attic. In that moment, the friar understood: **Cailleach** was older than time itself, an ancient force that had existed long before man could remember.

Her influence over the seasons is profound. In some stories, she rules the winter, while her counterpart, **Brigid**, reigns over the spring. The two are seen as opposing forces, each holding dominion over half of the year. But in other tales, they are not two separate goddesses at all. **Cailleach and Brigid are one and the same**, two sides of the same coin. As winter fades, **Cailleach** drinks from the **well of youth**, transforming herself into the vibrant, youthful **Brigid**. This transformation is the turning of the seasons, the shift from the cold stillness of winter to the blooming life of spring.

In another version of the myth, **Cailleach** does not transform but instead turns to **stone** at the end of winter, hiding her staff beneath a holly bush or a horse, waiting for the cold months to return. In these tales, she is linked to **death** — not just the death of the year but the death of souls. During the **winter solstice**, she rides through the skies with the **Wild Hunt**, gathering the souls of the dead, ensuring they do not linger in the world of the living.

To stand in the presence of **Cailleach** is to confront the inevitability of death and change. Yet, there is no cruelty in her actions. She is the force that moves the wheel of the seasons, the unseen hand that brings an end so that a new beginning can emerge. **Wayfarer**, if you find yourself drawn to her, know that she calls you to embrace the **cycles of life**, to understand that winter is not just an ending but the preparation for rebirth.

You may feel her presence in the wind, in the stillness of a frozen landscape, or in the wild howl of a wolf in the distance. She is a reminder that transformation is not always gentle — it can be fierce, cold, and untamed, but it is always necessary.

NORSE GODDESSESS

Wayfarer, can you hear the echo of ancient voices, those whose whispers call from the mists of time, summoning you to the **halls of Valhalla**? The Norse gods, fierce and wild, have woven their stories into the fabric of the land, the sea, and the sky. And within their tales lies not just the mighty thunder of Thor or the wisdom of Odin, but the power and mystery of the dark goddesses who dance in the shadows of their myths. They are the keepers of fate, the weavers of destiny, and the guardians of death—forces not to be feared but to be understood, embraced, and revered.

Yet the allure of Norse mythology goes beyond the battlefield. In the tales of these gods and goddesses, there is no clear division between light and dark. **Good** and **evil** are intertwined, just as the roots of Yggdrasil—the world tree—spread deep into the unknown realms. The **Norse deities** reflect the complexity of life itself: raw, untamed, and filled with contradictions. They are both creators and destroyers, protectors and harbingers of doom.

Among the shadows of Asgard, it is the **dark goddesses** who wield the most enigmatic power. To know them is to confront the mysteries of life and death, to stand on the precipice of understanding what lies beyond the veil.

Hela, the queen of the underworld, stands among these powerful figures. She rules over **Helheim**, the realm of the dead, where those who do not die in battle are sent. Her name alone brings a chill, for she is the one who presides over those forgotten by Valhalla. Half of her body is living flesh, while the other half is cold and lifeless—a visual reminder of the balance between life and death. She is not to be feared for her appearance, for she, like death itself, is simply a necessary part of existence. Her role is to guide the dead, to keep them, and to rule the underworld with an unyielding grip. But to invoke her is to invite the stark truth of mortality. If she calls to you, **wayfarer**, it is because she sees the courage in your heart to confront your own end and emerge with deeper wisdom.

In the folds of Norse myth, there are also the **Norns**, the ancient weavers of fate. These three sisters—**Urðr**, **Verdandi**, and **Skuld**—sit beneath the branches of Yggdrasil, spinning and cutting the threads of every life. Their power transcends even that of the gods, for not even Odin can escape his fate. To meet them is to glimpse the fabric of the cosmos, where every action, every choice, shapes the web of destiny. They are dark and mysterious, not because they are cruel, but because they operate in the space beyond human understanding. Their realm is time itself, ever-changing, ever-present. If they call to you, **wayfarer**, it is to remind you that your path is your own, yet it is also intricately woven into the greater tapestry of existence.

But it is not all death and fate. **Freyja**, the goddess of love, beauty, and war, stands on the threshold of both light and darkness. She rides across the sky in a chariot pulled by cats, a symbol of the sensual and the wild. Freyja leads half of those slain in battle to her hall, **Fólkvangr**, while the other half go to Valhalla. She is a goddess of contradictions, embodying both the nurturing aspects of love and the fierce, destructive power of war. In her eyes, there is both tenderness and untamed fury. When Freyja whispers your name, she calls you to embrace your full self—both the parts that love and the parts that rage.

Wayfarer, in this journey through the **Norse pantheon**, you will find that the line between light and dark is blurred. The goddesses of Asgard are neither purely good nor wholly evil. They embody the complexity of existence itself. The harsh winds of the **Norse winter** may bite at your flesh, but it is in this cold that true strength is found. **Hela, the Norns**, and **Freyja** each hold a piece of the truth, a truth that speaks to the cycles of life, death, and rebirth. And it is through their stories that you may find the **power** to unlock the secrets of your own spirit.

Here, in the heart of these ancient myths, where wolves howl in the night and ravens circle above the battlefield, lies a deeper understanding. These goddesses are more than legends; they are forces that dwell within you. They invite you to confront your fears, embrace your desires, and trust in the path that winds before you.

As you explore their stories, **wayfarer**, remember that they are not just tales of the past. They are echoes of the eternal struggle within each of us, between courage and fear, love and destruction, life and death.

Hel

Wayfarer, you find yourself on the edge of two worlds, caught between the realm of the living and the mysterious domain where souls are no longer bound by time. There, presiding over this dark threshold, stands a figure both feared and revered — **Hel**, goddess of the underworld, whose name has become synonymous with death itself. To know her is to understand the thin line between life and the inevitable, between existence and the deep unknown that lies beyond.

Hel, or **Hela**, bears a name that is also the name of her domain, a shadowed kingdom where the dead dwell. As the daughter of **Loki**, the trickster god, and the **giantess Angrboda**, Hel was born into a world of chaos and conflict. Her siblings, **Fenrir**, the wolf that would one day devour Odin, and **Jormungandr**, the world serpent who encircles Midgard, both echo the destructive nature of their lineage. Yet, it is **Hel** who takes on the solemn duty of tending to the souls of the departed, making her role both somber and sacred.

In her form, Hel embodies duality — half of her is like a giant, **blue and lifeless**, while the other half is like a mortal woman, **flesh-colored and alive**. This contrast symbolizes her dominion over two realms: the living and the dead. Her presence is a reminder that death is not separate from life, but part of its natural cycle. Some say she is cold and cruel, a ruler of shadows, while others whisper that she is beautiful in her ghostly way, with long, flowing hair and an ethereal grace.

Her kingdom, **Niflheim**, lies beneath the roots of Yggdrasil, the great World Tree. This frozen, mist-laden realm is often imagined as a place of cold, eternal stillness. For those who did not die gloriously in battle — and thus were denied entry to

Valhalla—Hel offered a different kind of peace. It was a realm for the old, the sick, and those who met their end not by sword but by the passage of time. Yet not all who dwell in Hel's kingdom find rest. The treacherous and cruel are sent to **Nastrond**, the Shore of Corpses, where their sins are repaid in full, their blood drained by the **dragon Nidhogg** as punishment.

But do not think Hel's realm to be only one of suffering, **wayfarer**. The underworld is a place of paradox, where Hel ensures balance between the living and the dead. For some, her kingdom is not a punishment but a reprieve. The weary, the frail, and the forgotten are sheltered in her embrace, far from the chaos of Midgard.

The origins of Hel's power are tied to the **prophecy** that her family would bring ruin to the gods of Asgard. When Odin, the All-Father, heard this, he sought to control the fate that threatened his realm. He cast her brother, **Jormungandr**, into the sea, where he would grow large enough to encircle the world. He chained **Fenrir**, fearing the wolf's strength would destroy them all. As for Hel, Odin banished her to the depths of Niflheim, offering her dominion over the dead as a way to contain her power. In this cold realm, she was told she would reign over all nine worlds—but this was Odin's deceit, for her true kingdom was only the land of the dead.

There, in the dark, Hel became queen. But she did not rebel against her fate; instead, she accepted it, growing into her power, commanding life and death, and controlling the flow of souls that passed through her domain. To cross her threshold is to submit to her rule, for Hel alone decides who enters and who leaves.

Wayfarer, Hel's powers are far-reaching. She holds dominion not only over the dead but also over the **balance between life and death**. She can summon the spirits of the fallen, and she alone has the ability to release a soul from the land of the dead. In this way, she is not an enemy of life but its caretaker, ensuring that the boundaries between the realms remain intact.

Some say that, like her father, Hel is a shapeshifter. She can appear as an eagle, a fox, or even a gust of wind. Her ability to take on different forms reminds us that death itself is a shapeshifter — coming to each person in a unique guise. But it is always there, waiting, patient, eternal.

In myth, **wayfarer**, Hel is often associated with certain symbols, each representing a facet of her power. The **spindle** she holds represents the thread of life and death, spun by the fates and cut when the time has come. A **sickle** hangs at her side, the tool used to reap life, mirroring her role as the bringer of death. And at the gates of her kingdom stands a **hound**, much like the Greek Cerberus, guarding the threshold between the worlds. Finally, the **serpent**, like her brother Jormungandr, symbolizes the endless cycle of death and rebirth, the shedding of skin, and the renewal of life in another realm.

Hel is often misunderstood, viewed through the lens of fear because of her connection to death. Yet death, in Norse mythology, is not evil. It is inevitable. To know Hel is to accept the cycle of life, death, and transformation. She is a **neutral force**, indifferent to the struggles of mortals, yet essential to their existence. Her cold embrace may seem harsh, but it is also fair — there is no escaping her domain, just as there is no escaping the final breath.

If you feel the call of Hel, **wayfarer**, it is because she invites you to confront your own fears of mortality, to embrace the parts of yourself that are often hidden, buried beneath the surface. Her realm is dark, yes, but within that darkness lies the truth that all things must end to begin again. The goddess of the underworld teaches us to accept the **shadow** as part of the whole, to face the inevitability of change, and to trust in the journey to the other side.

Hel, the **silent guardian** of the dead, watches over those who pass into her realm, ensuring that their stories do not end in despair, but continue in the quiet stillness of her domain. She is the keeper of the final secret, the one who knows what lies beyond the veil. And if you are brave enough to meet her gaze, **wayfarer**, you may find that death is not the end, but another step on the path to the unknown.

Skadi

Wayfarer, the cold winds of the northern mountains call to you, whispering tales of a fierce and powerful figure whose spirit roams the snowy peaks. **Skadi**, the giantess of winter, hunting, and mountains, is not a goddess born of Asgard, yet she commands as much respect as any deity. Her essence is not wrapped in softness or warmth, but in the harsh, biting winds of Jotunheim, the realm of giants. Skadi is a force of nature, not because of her lineage, but because she demanded to be heard, to be seen, and to be respected in the world of gods.

She hails from **Jotunheim**, where giants are often feared for their roughness, cruelty, and strength. But Skadi, despite her towering form and **blue skin**, was different. In a land where the fierce and fearsome reigned supreme, she stood out not only for her beauty but for her **unyielding nature**. It was said that no woman, mortal or divine, could match her prowess in skiing or hunting, and none could resist the harsh beauty she carried with her as easily as she carried her **quiver and bow**.

While most of the **Jotunn** were seen as adversaries of the gods, bringing war and chaos, Skadi's heart did not beat to that rhythm. She was **steady**, much like the mountains she so loved. Her strength, however, was not to be underestimated. She was calm but **unyielding**, fierce when wronged, but fair in her dealings.

Her story begins in vengeance. When her father, **Thiazi**, a giant of Jotunheim, was killed by the trickster god Loki, she knew her duty. Without hesitation, she donned her **armor**, her bow slung across her back, and made her way to **Asgard**, the land of the gods. She did not tremble before their might nor cower in the face of their divine power. She stood tall, demanding justice for the wrong done to her kin.

But the gods, ever wary of conflict, sought peace rather than bloodshed. They offered Skadi a deal—a marriage to one of their own, a way to unite her with their world. She agreed, but not without conditions. The gods were to **make her laugh**, a difficult task for beings so often consumed by duty and seriousness. Try as they might, they failed to bring joy to the stoic giantess, until **Loki**, ever the schemer, tied a rope to a goat's beard and the other end to his private parts. The goat's jerky movements and Loki's high-pitched yelps finally drew a laugh from Skadi, and with that, the pact was sealed.

The next step in their bargain required her to choose a husband—but she could only choose by looking at the feet of the gods. Skadi, her heart already swayed by the thought of the **handsome Balder**, searched for the most beautiful feet, certain they belonged to him. But when the veil was lifted, she found herself staring into the eyes of **Njord**, the god of the sea, much older and far removed from the ethereal beauty of Balder.

Skadi and Njord were as different as the lands they ruled—one bound to the sea, the other to the icy mountains. They tried to make their marriage work, dividing their time between Njord's **coastal hall**, where the sound of waves lulled him to sleep, and Skadi's **snowy peaks**, where the wind howled through the rocks and the wolves roamed freely. But nine days in the mountains were unbearable for Njord, and nine days by the sea made Skadi long for the cold embrace of the winter wind. In time, they parted ways, but there was no bitterness, only the understanding that not all unions are meant to last.

Though her marriage ended, Skadi's story did not. Her independence, her fierceness, and her connection to the natural world made her a figure of admiration. She ruled the mountains as a **solitary queen**, a huntress on skis, bow always at the ready, her heart as cold and unforgiving as the snow she traversed. Some tales suggest that she found a better match in **Ullr**, the god of skiing and hunting, sharing her love for the winter wilderness. Others claim she took **Odin** as a lover, bearing him children who carried her legacy of strength and resolve.

Yet, Skadi was not merely a figure of beauty or revenge. She was a survivor, a giantess who had earned her place among the gods, even after her father's betrayal and death. Her loyalty to her father's memory did not prevent her from finding her own path, nor did it blind her to the complexities of life among the gods. She even stood with the gods during **Ragnarok**, the twilight of the gods, when she fought alongside them against the forces of chaos. She was not a creature of vengeance alone—she was a protector, a ruler, and, above all, **a survivor**.

Skadi's name carries deep meaning. Some say it stems from the word **"Skadi"**, meaning harm or shadow, reflecting her giantess origins, where darkness and destruction were often attributed to her kind. Others argue that her name might have inspired the name of **Scandinavia**, a land that embodies her harsh, cold beauty. Whether she was a goddess or a giantess was irrelevant to those who revered her, for they prayed to her, asking for mercy in the harsh winters and protection during hunts in the frozen mountains.

Her symbols were simple but powerful—the **bow and arrow**, representing her unmatched skill as a huntress; her **snow shoes**, a sign of her mastery of the wild, icy landscapes; and the **wolf**, her constant companion, representing her bond with the wild creatures of the mountains.

In the end, **wayfarer**, Skadi's story is one of resilience and independence. She is not defined by her losses—her father's death or her failed marriage—but by her ability to carve out a place for herself, to demand respect and to stand firm in the face of adversity. She is the embodiment of the **untamed wild**, the cold wind that bites but also sustains, the mountain peak that seems unreachable but offers the most magnificent view to those who dare to climb it.

So when the cold winds blow, and the mountains call your name, think of **Skadi** — the goddess who walks among the wolves, her bow at the ready, her heart unshaken. She teaches you to embrace the harshness, to find beauty in the struggle, and to know that even in the most desolate of winters, there is strength and resilience to be found. **You, too, can master the mountains**.

Angrboda

Wayfarer, as you traverse the forests of forgotten myths and listen to the echoes of long-buried stories, you will come across a name that lingers in the shadows — **Angrboda**, the mother of monsters, the giantess who dwelled in the heart of Ironwood. Her name alone carries the weight of destiny, translating to "the one who brings grief," or "distress bringer." And grief, indeed, followed her wherever her tale is told, for her children would one day bring about the twilight of the gods.

Angrboda's origins are rooted deep in **Jotunheim**, the land of the giants. Unlike the beautiful gods of Asgard, the Jotunn were often depicted as rough, fierce, and terrifying in form, yet Angrboda's presence transcended mere appearance. With **blood-red hair**, **bluish skin**, and the raw power of the giants coursing through her veins, she was a force of nature in her own right. The forest where she lived, **Ironwood**, was a dark and mystical place, home to female giants, where secrets were whispered among the trees, and prophecies of doom took shape in the cold, stony earth. The **monsters** she bore to Loki were not mere creatures — they were embodiments of chaos and the unraveling of the cosmos. **Fenrir**, the wolf destined to devour the sun; **Jormungandr**, the serpent who encircled the world; and **Hel**, the queen of the underworld who would shepherd souls into her dark realm. To birth such beings was to carry the weight of worlds in her womb. **You cannot bear the destroyers of gods without being forged from something darker, something more powerful than most could comprehend.**

Despite her monstrous offspring, there was more to Angrboda than the chaos she mothered. She was a **seeress**, gifted with the sight of things to come, able to look deep into the threads of fate. It was said that she could **decipher the runes**, those ancient symbols of destiny and power, and her knowledge of **magic** was vast, rivaling even that of Odin himself. Like her lover Loki, she had the ability to **shapeshift**, a power that allowed her to move unseen through the realms, taking the form of wolves, birds, or even the mist that curled through the dark trees of Ironwood.

But it was her relationship with **Loki** that stirred the most conflict. Their love was real, passionate, and wild. The trickster god, known for his slippery loyalties and ever-shifting nature, found in Angrboda a kindred spirit, a companion who shared his hunger for rebellion and destruction. Yet, even as he fathered her children, his place in Asgard became more tenuous. The gods feared the giantess, for they knew the destiny that came with her and her offspring. The future she carried in her blood terrified them. **Odin**, ever cautious, ever watchful, knew he could not let the children of Angrboda grow unchecked. He feared their power—rightly so. And so he sent his son **Thor** to capture the giantess and bring her to Asgard. The god of thunder, mighty in his own right, managed to take her from Ironwood, and in Asgard's golden halls, she faced the gods who would demand her greatest sacrifice.

The gods knew they could not kill her, for her magic was too powerful, her connection to fate too deep. Instead, they struck a bargain. **Her freedom** in exchange for **her children**. And though her heart ached, Angrboda agreed, for she knew the wheels of destiny had already begun to turn.

Fenrir was bound in chains upon an island, his howls echoing through the realms. **Jormungandr** was cast into the sea, his body growing so vast that he could encircle the world itself. And **Hel** was sent to the underworld, where she would rule over the dead. But these measures, taken by Odin in fear, would not prevent the coming of **Ragnarok**, the end of all things.

In the final battle, **Ragnarok**, Angrboda's children would rise to fulfill their destiny. **Fenrir**, the great wolf, would break free from his chains and devour the sun, plunging the world into darkness. He would face Odin in battle, and in that terrible clash, Fenrir would **swallow the All-Father whole**. **Jormungandr** would rise from the depths, spitting venom and destruction as he battled Thor. And **Hel**, with her army of the dead, would march from the underworld to join the fight. It was the end of the world as the gods knew it.

And what of Angrboda herself? Some say she fought alongside her children, her heart burning with the grief and fury that had been her constant companions. Others claim that she vanished, her fate lost in the chaos of the world's end. But one thing is certain—**her legacy** lived on in the destruction her children wrought, and in the new world that rose from the ashes of the old.

As you, **wayfarer**, journey deeper into the dark forests of mythology, **Angrboda** stands as a reminder of the power that comes from embracing chaos and the inevitability of fate. She is a figure of **strength**, of **magic**, and of **deep sorrow**, a giantess whose story, though not as well-known as others, is just as powerful. Her children shaped the world, but she shaped them, and through them, she lives on.

In her, you will find the embodiment of **transformation**, the mother of those forces that bring change—violent, unstoppable change. **To walk in her footsteps is to understand that sometimes, destruction is necessary for renewal, that the darkest paths often lead to the most profound truths.**

When you hear the wolves howl, or when you dream of serpents rising from the deep, think of **Angrboda**. She is there, in the shadows, watching, waiting, knowing that in the end, **chaos always has its place**.

SUMMON İNNER GODDESS

Wayfarer, as you journey deeper into the hidden realms of your soul, this chapter invites you to embrace the Dark Goddess within—a powerful guide to unlocking the shadow self and awakening the divine feminine energy that lies dormant within you. This is not a journey for the faint-hearted, for the **Dark Goddess** is a mirror, reflecting both your deepest fears and your untapped power.

The **Dark Goddess** that resides within you is not something to be feared, but rather a force to be embraced. Society often teaches us to suppress the darker aspects of ourselves, to hide our shadows beneath the surface. But those shadows, those imperfections, are the very keys to your empowerment. To deny them is to deny a part of your soul.

Many feel a pull toward this shadow energy, but it can be unsettling at first—this draw to something that feels both mysterious and familiar. Yet, **the darkness within you is not destructive by nature**, it is a part of your wholeness. **Your shadow** can serve as a beacon of transformation, guiding you through spiritual growth and leading you to a deeper understanding of your true self.

When the **Dark Goddess** begins to stir within you, you may notice her subtle manifestations in your daily life. Perhaps you've been feeling more insecure, **doubting yourself in ways that feel overwhelming**. Or maybe you've felt a surge of envy or a deep-seated fear of rejection, as though your worth is being questioned. These emotions, while uncomfortable, are signs that the goddess within is awakening, urging you to confront the shadow parts of yourself you've kept hidden.

You may find yourself striving for perfection, overly sensitive to the opinions of others, or reacting strongly when your boundaries are crossed. These are all signs that the **goddess** is calling you to do the deep work of self-discovery, asking you to look at the parts of yourself that need healing and nurturing.

Acknowledge these feelings, wayfarer, for they are not your enemies. They are the gifts of the goddess, a reminder that even in your darkest moments, there is power waiting to be unearthed.

The shadow is not something to be conquered, but rather something to be integrated. By embracing the Dark Goddess within, you are beginning the process of acknowledging your shadow self — a crucial step in this spiritual journey. The **goddess** is not separate from you; she is woven into the very fabric of your being, and her power comes alive when you dare to confront the parts of yourself that you've been taught to hide.

There are many ways to approach this work, **but it is not something you can rush**. Some may find meditation a powerful tool, as it allows you to sit in stillness, to breathe deeply and focus on the darker emotions that bubble up within you. In these moments of silence, the **goddess** whispers, inviting you to listen to the truths you've been avoiding.

Other practices, like shadow work, are equally profound. Here, you delve into the darker aspects of your personality — those emotional triggers, destructive behaviors, and hidden desires that you've pushed away. Through shadow work, you can bring these pieces into the light, transforming them into something that serves your highest good. **As you uncover these hidden parts**, you'll begin to see the wisdom they carry. You'll no longer fear your imperfections, but instead, recognize them as powerful allies on your path to wholeness.

The process of **shadow integration** is not an easy one, wayfarer. It requires patience, compassion, and a willingness to explore the uncharted territories of your mind and soul. But it is through this work that you will come to understand the full depth of the Dark Goddess's power within you. By bringing your shadow self out of the unconscious, you will harness the darkness that once controlled you and instead use it as a tool to navigate the world with clarity and purpose.

The **Dark Goddess** teaches us that to truly know ourselves, we must accept every aspect of who we are—**light and dark, joy and sorrow, love and anger**. In this space, you will find **your deepest truths**, those that lie beneath the surface of your everyday thoughts and emotions. By connecting with your **inner goddess**, you open the door to transformation, to a life where your power is not diminished by fear, but enhanced by the integration of your shadow.

The more you embrace the dark feminine, the more you will see how her energy flows through you. You will no longer shy away from your emotions, no matter how intense they may be. Instead, you will wield them with intention, **allowing yourself to feel deeply and live authentically**.

Wayfarer, this is not a path to be rushed, but one that must be walked with reverence and awareness. As you move forward, remember that the Dark Goddess is always there, waiting within you. **She is not separate from you; she is you**, the embodiment of your shadow and your light, your fear and your strength.

Let her guide you into the depths, and in doing so, you will emerge transformed. **The journey to embracing the Dark Goddess is not one of destruction, but one of rebirth.** And as you embrace her, you will find the empowerment you've been seeking, a power that comes not from the denial of your shadow, but from the integration of every part of who you are.

In the quiet moments, in the stillness of your mind, **listen for her call**. She is always there, waiting to show you the path to wholeness, if only you have the courage to follow her into the darkness. **Embrace her, wayfarer, and you will embrace the fullness of your soul.**

Shadow Visualization exercise

Wayfarer, let this be your guide as you embark on a journey inward, into the shadowy depths of your soul. The **Dark Goddess** calls you to meet your shadow self, not with fear, but with curiosity and openness. This visualization is a tool, a sacred invitation to integrate the forgotten or repressed parts of yourself. **Take your time, for this is not a path to be rushed.**

First, seek out a quiet space where the world outside fades, where your attention will not be pulled away. **Sit or lie down comfortably** and close your eyes, letting the stillness settle around you.

Breathe in deeply through your mouth, feeling the air fill your lungs, and **exhale gently through your nostrils,** releasing tension with each breath. **Do not rush.** At first, your mind may feel restless, a dance of thoughts swirling in the background. **Allow them to move freely without judgment,** like clouds passing across the sky.

As you inhale, feel your body softening. Let go of any tightness. If the quiet seems elusive, don't force it—let it come naturally. **Perhaps the sound of soft meditation music or the scent of burning incense can help guide you deeper into relaxation.**

Now, as your body rests, **see yourself standing at the entrance of a dark cave.** The air here is thick, cool, and alive with mystery. This is no ordinary cave. It is the cave of your **shadow self**, the hidden aspects of your soul, waiting to be uncovered.

Step forward, wayfarer. As you enter, feel the chill of the air wrap around you like a veil, yet do not fear it. With each step, the darkness embraces you, and you walk deeper into the unknown, guided only by instinct.

In the distance, you notice a faint flicker — **a tiny light**, fragile yet unwavering. **Walk toward it.** This light is your beacon, and as you approach, its glow reveals a shadowy figure standing just beyond the flame.

Here, in this place of shadows, you can feel their presence — dark yet familiar, powerful yet inviting. **You feel both drawn to and hesitant of this figure.** Pause for a moment and listen to your body. **Where does this feeling settle?** In your chest, your stomach, your throat? **Let yourself feel the weight of this ambiguity without rushing to define it.**

When you're ready, **step closer**. The figure is not here to harm you. They are here to reveal what you have hidden, to show you what lies beneath the surface.

Ask them who they are. Ask them what they wish to tell you, or what they want to show you. **Do not be afraid of their answers.** You might feel their words as much as you hear them, a truth that resonates deep within you. **This shadow is part of you,** a reflection of something you've long tried to suppress. Perhaps it is a forgotten memory, a fear you've buried, or a truth you've denied yourself.

Listen carefully. **Take note of the message they bring.** It may feel unsettling, but know that you are safe here. You don't need to embrace everything all at once. **Only take what you are ready to handle.** There will be more time to return if needed.

When you feel the conversation is complete, or when you sense that you've received all you can for now, let the shadow begin to **fade into the darkness**. But know this — what they have revealed will remain with you, ready for further exploration when you are willing.

This is only the beginning, wayfarer. Each time you return to this cave, new layers of your shadow will reveal themselves. The

Dark Goddess walks with you on this path, offering you the strength to face what you've hidden, to embrace the full scope of who you are.

With time and practice, you will learn to carry this shadow, not as a burden, but as a **source of wisdom and power**. This journey will unfold as you continue to meet the parts of yourself long forgotten, and through this practice, you will move closer to embracing the **Dark Goddess** within.

Awakening Your Inner Dark Goddess

Wayfarer, step into the embrace of the **Dark Goddess**. This chapter guides you deeper into her mysteries, offering practices that will awaken your inner power and reveal the shadow self that waits beneath the surface. Each practice is an invitation—a ritual to connect, a path to knowing yourself more fully, even in the parts you've long hidden.

The influence of the **Dark Goddess** whispers through the trees, stirs in the waters, and dances on the winds. **Her energy is woven into every element of nature.** Whether you walk barefoot on damp earth or listen to the quiet ripple of a stream, you are touching her essence.

Take every opportunity to let nature speak to you, even if it's just a moment in the grass, beneath the shade of a tree. If you live near the water, let the waves carry your thoughts as you call on the goddess. If you are bound to the city, surround yourself with plants, stones, and crystals—create your sanctuary where her presence can thrive. **Feel her in the stillness, in the rain, in the moonlight.**

As you walk this path, journaling becomes an act of discovery. **It's more than writing—it's a dialogue with your inner darkness.** When you put pen to paper, let the thoughts flow without restriction. **Write your truth, even when it feels uncomfortable.** Each word you write reveals a part of you that longs to be seen.

Record your experiences, your dreams, your shadows. Reflect at the end of the week and see what patterns emerge. **You might be surprised by what your soul whispers when you're willing to listen.** Even when you don't know where to start, let your pen move. You'll find there's much more beneath the surface than you realized.

To embrace your shadow self is to embrace **all** of you—**your imperfections, your fears, your desires.** The **Dark Goddess** knows the power in loving every part of your being, even the parts that feel too wild, too broken, or too dark to love. **Show yourself kindness,** for self-love is a sacred act of reclaiming all that you are.

Accept your past. Release what no longer serves you. **In loving yourself, you signal that you are ready to integrate every aspect of your being.** You are not too much. You are enough—every flaw, every fear, every shadow. By offering yourself love, you open the door to the Dark Goddess within.

The dark moon holds profound magic. It is the time when the night sky is at its deepest, when the energy of the Dark Goddess pulses strongest. **In this meditation, you will journey into that darkness** and awaken her within.

Find a quiet place, wayfarer, and settle in. Let the world fade away as you sink into the moment. Close your eyes and take a deep breath, letting it fill your body completely before releasing it slowly.

Picture yourself standing at the edge of a dark, ancient forest. **Follow your instinct** as you step into the trees. The branches overhead weave a canopy of shadows, but you walk with confidence, knowing that this path leads to the depths of your soul. **There is no need for fear here—this is sacred ground.**

As you walk, you come upon a clearing. There is a fire burning, the flames crackling softly, casting flickering light on the earth. **Settle in front of the fire and focus your thoughts.** With each breath, feel yourself becoming grounded. Your breath travels up to your crown, down to your feet, and into the earth beneath you. **You are connected—both to the dark energy within and to the earth itself.**

Feel the energy around you expand, encircling the clearing, creating a sanctuary. **Here, nothing can harm you.** You are safe, cradled by the energy of the earth and the Dark Goddess.

Now, let your thoughts turn to the months ahead. **Feel the energy of your desires, your plans, your hopes.** Channel these into the fire. **What do these dreams mean to you?** How will they transform your life? Sit with these thoughts and let the flames absorb them, feeding the energy of your future.

As the fire burns, the clearing fades away. **You are surrounded by darkness now.** There is no fear, only quiet. The subtle glow of the dark moon lights your path, guiding you deeper into the mystery.

Let go. Let go of your fears, your doubts, the limitations you've placed on yourself. **In this darkness, there is freedom.** You are connected to the unknown, to the great mystery, to the dark feminine within.

Feel her rise in your heart, her energy merging with your own. She is the truth you carry—the power to speak your truth, to live it boldly. **Let the energy rise, from your heart to the stars, filling you with strength.**

When you are ready, breathe deeply once more. **Let the images dissolve** and return to the present. But know this—**you have awakened something within.** You are no longer afraid of the unknown. **The Dark Goddess walks with you now, guiding you through the shadows, and empowering you to reclaim all that is yours.**

ADVANCED RITUALS

Wayfarer, if you have found yourself drawn to this chapter, you are on the precipice of a deeper, more transformative path — one where you will step into the shadows and encounter the raw, primal energy of the Dark Goddess. This is not a path for the faint-hearted, nor one for those who seek quick answers. The ritual you are about to undertake is both potent and perilous, designed to connect your soul with the essence of the **Dark Goddess.**

Be warned, this ritual opens a gateway between the material and the spiritual realms, where shadows dance and forgotten truths emerge. It is a place where the Dark Goddess reigns, her energy potent and untamed. She does not appear without demand, and once summoned, she will see through to the depths of your soul.

Proceed with caution, for to invoke her is to invite her powerful, sometimes dangerous, presence into your life. She brings transformation, but often through destruction, facing you with your deepest fears, hidden desires, and unresolved shadows.

Preparation of the Self

Before you step into her domain, you must first **prepare yourself completely — both in body and spirit**. The energy you seek to invoke is primal and vast, untamed and fiercely transformative. **To enter into this space unprepared would be folly**, for the Dark Goddess does not tolerate anything less than your whole self.

Purification is the first step, not just of the body but of the soul. Every ritual of magic, every invocation of ancient energies, requires that you cleanse yourself of the mundane. **You are to stand skyclad — naked — before her.** There is no place for ego here, no room for the illusions we wrap ourselves in for protection. **To remove your clothing is to remove those masks** — the layers of ego, fear, and control. The Dark Goddess, in her wisdom, sees through every pretense, every shield you've built around your heart and soul. **There is no hiding from her.**

Before you invoke her, **there is one more sacred boundary** to heed. **Do not perform this ritual during your moon time.** The blood of your menstrual cycle, while a powerful current of life in its own right, will interfere with the delicate balance of energies this ritual demands.

The physical flow of your life blood mingles with the spiritual flow of the Dark Goddess, and if summoned while you are bleeding, her energy may become volatile, uncontrollable.

The Dark Goddess, though fierce, commands respect for her power. She will not be summoned lightly, and certainly not when the energies within you are misaligned. Only proceed when you are fully attuned, in harmony with your body, spirit, and mind.

The Dark Goddess calls for you in your most open, vulnerable, and receptive state.

This is not a warning to discourage you, but a reminder of the **sacred contract** you are entering into. She will meet you where you are—**but you must be ready to stand unflinchingly in her presence**.

The Circle of the Four Towers

Wayfarer, you are about to step into a space where the veils are thin, where the air hums with the energy of the unseen. **Now, trace your circle.** This is your sanctuary and your gateway, the boundary that holds both **protection and power**. As you trace this sacred space, you are not merely marking the ground; you are carving out a **realm between worlds**, a place where time bends, where the Dark Goddess listens. Every movement you make must be intentional, steady, deliberate. **The circle is your bridge between the mundane and the mystical**, and within it, you will invite forces that have roamed the shadows for centuries.

Begin by gathering the tools that will anchor this ritual. **You need four candles, dark in hue,** each carrying the ancient essence of the elements, but not in the way you have known them. These candles hold within them a deeper current, a darker pulse that resonates with the energy of the Dark Goddess.

The black candle calls upon Earth, but not the nurturing soil of spring. This is the earth that has known death and decay, the **rich black soil** from which all things eventually return. It is the fertile darkness, the cradle of bones, the cold, solid ground that shelters what lies beneath. Place this candle in the North, where the **earth rests firm and cold**, and feel the weight of the element grounding you, pulling your energy deep.

The purple candle summons Air, but not the gentle breeze or light winds. This is the **breath of storms**, the air thick with ancient whispers and unsolved mysteries, the force that stirs in the dead of night when secrets pass from lip to lip. It belongs in the East, the direction of first light, but here the dawn is cloaked in shadow. As you place this candle, feel the air thicken around you, charged with potential, waiting to reveal what has long been hidden.

Next, take the **brown (or dark blue or dark green) candle to invoke Water**. This is not the playful, rippling water of clear rivers. This is the water that lies still in darkened pools, the unseen depths of the ocean where no light dares to venture. It is the slow, transformative current that carves its path over time, hidden but strong. Set it in the West, where the sun dips low and the shadows lengthen, bringing with them the promise of transformation.

Finally, place the **dark red candle to call upon Fire**. But this is no comforting hearth flame. **This is the fire that destroys**, the blaze that strips away all pretense, leaving only truth in its wake. It is the inferno that purifies, that burns through illusion and lies, forcing all to reveal their raw essence. Set this candle in the South, where the heat of transformation burns brightest, and feel the flames rising within you, challenging you to release what no longer serves.

Now, **move clockwise around the circle**, lighting each candle as you pass. Let the flames flicker and dance in the dark, casting long shadows that stretch toward the center of your circle. **As the fire touches the wick, speak aloud, calling on the elements to rise and witness, to protect and empower:**

"By the black earth beneath, the purple air above, the brown waters that flow deep, and the red fire that burns within — I call the towers to rise. Guard this circle. Seal this space. Let no force enter but by my will and the will of the Dark Goddess."

As the words leave your lips, **feel the elements stir**. The earth beneath your feet seems to solidify, grounding you deeper into the ritual. The air thickens, charged with electricity, the promise of secrets unveiled. The water pulls, slow and deep, stirring emotions and transformations yet unseen. The fire crackles and grows, consuming all that is false, leaving nothing but truth in its wake.

The circle is now drawn. You stand at the center of a sacred boundary, sealed by the ancient forces you have called upon. **The Four Towers rise around you**, sentinels of earth, air, water, and fire, their energies intertwining to create a space where only truth and power may enter.

Stay within this circle, and know that from this moment on, you are no longer alone. The Dark Goddess is near, watching from the edges of your sacred space, waiting for the moment you are ready to meet her gaze.

The Triangle of Summoning

Wayfarer, as you step deeper into this sacred space, it is now time to **invoke the Triangle of Summoning**, the conduit through which the Dark Goddess will pass from her shadowed realm into your circle. This triangle is not just a symbol or geometric shape; it is a **divine vessel**, a key that unlocks the doorway between worlds. It creates a space where energies converge, where light and shadow entwine, and where the Goddess herself may manifest.

Gather three **small gray candles**, for gray is the hue of the in-between, a color that exists neither in full light nor in darkness but in the spaces where the two meet. This is the place of mystery, the liminal, the threshold between worlds where the shadows walk, and whispers linger. You will use these candles to **form the sacred triangle** — a container strong enough to hold the immense energy of the Dark Goddess. Kneel at the center of your circle, the air already thick with the power of the Four Towers. With steady hands, place the gray candles in the form of a triangle at the very heart of the space. **Feel the weight of your intention settle in** as you do so. This triangle will become the **cradle of the Goddess's presence**, a vessel to hold her energy as it descends.

Now, take a piece of **parchment**, pure and blank, and prepare to write the name of the Goddess you seek to summon. You must write her name in the **Theban script**, the ancient alphabet of witches. Do this with **red ink**, for red is the color of life, of blood, of the sacrifices we make on this journey. As the red flows from your pen, **feel the ink binding you to the Goddess**, sealing your intent with a thread of energy that stretches between you and her unseen form. **The words you write hold power**, for in them you call her forth, summoning her from the depths of the unseen.

Place the parchment carefully within the triangle of candles. **It is a sacred offering**, a message cast into the abyss, waiting for her to answer. The name you have inscribed is no mere word — it is a key, a gateway through which her presence will flow. It holds the weight of ancient mysteries, and by placing it at the triangle's heart, you are opening the path for her to step forward.

a   b   c   d   e   f   g   h

i   k   l   m   n   o   p   q

r   s   t   v   x   y   3   w

Next, you must light the summoning incense. The incense should be a blend of **charcoal and dry spices** — materials that carry the resonance of earth and fire, of transformation and purity. As you light the incense, **watch the smoke rise** in curling tendrils, twisting and turning as it ascends into the air. **The smoke is your offering**, the bridge between the mortal and divine. It carries your will upward, into the realms that lie beyond your circle, beyond the sight of human eyes. **Let it carry your intent like a whispered plea**, delicate but resolute, spiraling through the unseen spaces that connect this world to the one where the Dark Goddess dwells.

As the scent fills the air, the atmosphere around you will begin to change. The flames of the gray candles may flicker, responding to the energy you have invoked. The space inside your circle will feel heavier, the air thick with anticipation. **You are not alone** here, not anymore. The Dark Goddess listens, and soon, you will feel her presence stir.

Allow yourself to sink into the **ritual's energy**, surrendering to the pull of the smoke and the fire, the scent and the silence. Your heart may race, but do not fear. **She will come in her own time**, when the veil between worlds has thinned enough to allow her passage.

And as you wait, attune your senses. **Feel the shift in the air**, the subtle trembling of the ground beneath your feet. The Dark Goddess is approaching, drawn to the summoning you have carefully crafted. **Her essence lingers on the edges of your awareness**, a shadow at the corner of your vision, a presence you cannot yet fully see but can already feel deep in your soul. **You are no longer waiting; you are becoming part of the summoning itself**.

This is the moment before her arrival, the pause before the storm. Stay grounded in your circle, for the energy here is wild, ancient, and potent. **You are now standing at the threshold**, the point where worlds collide, where you and the Goddess will meet.

Her arrival will not be gentle. She is the Dark Goddess, after all, and her presence will **challenge you**—but it will also transform you. Stay with her, wayfarer, for you have already come this far. **Trust in the ritual, trust in the space you have created**, and trust in the connection you have summoned.

The Ritual Space

Wayfarer, you have come this far, and now the true work begins. As you prepare to delve even deeper into the realm of shadow, **heed the symbols you are about to place** within your circle, for they are not mere objects, but sacred tools — each with its own energy, each a gateway into the unknown.

At the **northernmost point** of your circle, take the **white candle** into your hands. This candle, though it burns with a white flame, is not a symbol of light as you may know it. It is the **purifying fire** — a flame that will burn away fear and hesitation, creating a shield around you as you journey deeper into the dark realms. **Feel the wax between your fingers** as you place it down, sensing the power it holds, a reminder that even in the shadow, there is protection. **Its flame dances not in defiance of the dark**, but as a guide through it, ensuring your safety as you confront the unknown.

Now, at the **southernmost point**, opposite the white flame, place the **obsidian mirror**. This is no ordinary mirror, wayfarer. It is forged from the heart of volcanic fire, born from the very belly of the earth — **a creation of raw, elemental energy**. Obsidian is the stone of transformation, a reflection not only of the outer world but of your innermost shadows. **It will not lie to you**, nor will it coddle you. It is a portal, a gateway through which the Dark Goddess will reveal herself. Place it with reverence, knowing that once you look into its depths, you may never see yourself the same way again.

When the mirror and the candle are set, you are ready to enter the **space between them** — the space that holds both shadow and light, fear and courage, truth and illusion. **Stand at the center of your circle**, between the white flame of protection and the obsidian mirror of shadow. You are now the bridge, wayfarer, between the material and the spiritual, the seen and the unseen.

Close your eyes and take a deep breath. Feel the weight of the air around you—the way it thickens, as if infused with the energy of the Four Towers and the power of the Triangle you have summoned. Let your breath anchor you, drawing you deeper into the circle's energy. **With each inhale**, feel the energy rising from the earth beneath your feet, filling you, grounding you. **With each exhale**, sense the presence of the Dark Goddess growing closer, as though she is drawn to your call, pulled into the space you have created.

Her energy is not soft, wayfarer. **It is wild and untamed**, swirling through the smoke of the incense, flickering in the flames of the candles. You can feel her now, can't you? **A presence, a force**—both familiar and terrifying. She is not here to comfort you, but to **show you the truths you've hidden from yourself**, to make you face the shadows that dwell within. **Her energy spirals through you**, filling the circle, making the air thick with her power. You are standing at the edge of something immense, something that will transform you if you allow it.

But do not look to the mirror yet. Not until you are ready.

Breathe again, deeper this time. Feel the obsidian beneath your feet, the stone of transformation, solid and unyielding. Let its energy flow upward, anchoring you to the earth even as the presence of the Dark Goddess begins to swirl around you, **her essence merging with the air, the earth, the fire, and the water of your circle**. She is close now, her power so palpable that it feels as if the shadows themselves are alive, **moving, breathing**, waiting for the moment when you will look into the mirror and see her—see yourself—in a way you have never done before.

This is the moment of **stillness before the storm**, the calm before the Dark Goddess reveals herself fully. You are on the precipice, wayfarer, standing between what you know and what you fear. **Do not rush** this moment. Let it linger. Let the energy build, like a wave gathering force, preparing to break.

When you are ready, open your eyes and **turn toward the obsidian mirror. Feel its pull**, the way it calls to you, beckoning you to look into its depths. But know this: **what you see reflected in the mirror is not just your outer form**, but the reflection of your shadow self, the parts of you that have been hidden, forgotten, perhaps even feared. The Dark Goddess **will reveal herself through this mirror**, but she will also reveal you — **the truths that lie beneath the surface, the fears you've buried, the desires you've denied.**

Step forward, wayfarer. **Gaze into the mirror. Let her eyes meet yours**. You are ready.

The Invocation of the Dark Goddess

Wayfarer, you are ready now, aligned in both body and mind. **The air thickens around you**, vibrating with the energy you have summoned, and now it is time to speak the sacred names of the Dark Goddess. These names are ancient, each one a key, unlocking the door that stands between this world and the shadowed realms where she dwells. But know this—you do not command her. You cannot force her hand. You are calling to her, inviting her into your space, your life, your very soul.

Your voice must carry the weight of your intent. **Feel the energy rise within you** as you prepare to speak. The jacula, the ancient invocatory prayer, is more than a string of words—it is an incantation, a vibration that will resonate through the circle, through the triangle of summoning, and beyond. As you begin to chant, each name is like a drumbeat, drawing her closer.

"Lilith... Morrigan... Hekate... Kali... Lilith... Morrigan... Hekate... Kali..."

Feel the power of these names within you. With every repetition, **you stir the air**, and the circle becomes charged. The energy builds with each breath, with each invocation. You are no longer simply speaking—**you are channeling**. These are not just words; they are doorways, and each goddess you name holds the key to a different part of the divine feminine's shadow, a different face of power, wisdom, and destruction.

The vibrations of the chant **echo in your bones**, reverberating through your entire being. The candles flicker, their flames dancing in rhythm to the growing energy. And now, wayfarer, **turn your eyes to the obsidian mirror**. What do you see? At first, there may be nothing but darkness, shadows that shift and swirl. **But do not look away**. Keep your gaze steady, for this is where the Dark Goddess will reveal herself. She may come as a shadowy figure, as a raven perched at the edge of the mirror, or as a woman cloaked in darkness, her form only partially visible.

The image may shift, fluid and elusive, but **her presence will grow stronger**. You will feel it, like a weight pressing against your chest, against your very soul. **She is here**. And when your eyes meet hers, you will know. You have opened the door, and she has stepped through.

The Dark Goddess does not come without challenge. **Her gaze will strip away your pretenses**. She sees you for what you truly are, and she will show you what you need to see, even if it is what you have long avoided. **Breathe, wayfarer. Do not shrink from this moment**. Let her energy wash over you, fill the space, penetrate your being. This is why you called her — to face what has been hidden, to confront the shadow.

Her presence will test you. You may feel an overwhelming surge of emotions — fear, pain, anger, sorrow. She brings these things to the surface, not to break you, but to make you stronger, to prepare you for transformation. This is the power of the Dark Goddess. **She does not hide from the truth**, and neither must you.

Feel her power filling the circle. It spirals around you, through the triangle of summoning, into the very core of your being. **You are no longer separate from her**. Her energy flows through you, and you through her. The boundaries between you and the Dark Goddess blur, merging into one. **This is the connection you sought**. This is the awakening you longed for.

Stay with her for as long as you can. Allow her to show you what you need to see, to guide you through the labyrinth of your own soul. She will not leave until her work is done, until you have faced the shadows within. **But know this**, wayfarer — once you have invited her into your life, she will remain with you, even after the ritual is complete. **Her presence lingers**, a reminder of the journey you have begun, the transformation that lies ahead.

When you are ready, and only when you are ready, **you may release her**. But the Dark Goddess will always be with you now, her essence woven into the fabric of your being. You are no longer the same. You have seen her, and in doing so, you have seen yourself.

Banishment and Closing

Wayfarer, now that the Dark Goddess has revealed herself and whispered her truths into your soul, it is time to carefully close the ritual. Her presence, powerful and raw, must be released with intention, or else it may linger in ways you do not yet understand. Her energy, if left untethered, can disturb the very balance you sought to create.

Feel the weight of her presence fading slightly, yet she remains near, waiting for you to complete the process. In your hand, take the white candle — this is your final act of protection, the flame that burns away the lingering shadows, sealing the gateway. Hold it high above you, and speak the words that will guide her back to her realm:

"Dark Goddess, I thank you for your presence. I release you now to your realm. Go in peace, as I remain."

The air shifts as you speak, your voice carrying both gratitude and command. Blow out the white candle, watching as the flame flickers for a final moment before disappearing into smoke. **This simple breath closes the gateway**, marking the end of her passage into your world. The connection begins to dissolve.

Now, turn your attention to the obsidian mirror. **Its surface, once alive with her essence, is now still.** Gently, without haste, cover the mirror with a black cloth. This cloth is more than a covering — it seals the portal, ensuring that nothing more passes through. **The darkness behind the mirror remains behind it.** You are closing the door, but not forever.

Feel the shift in energy, a subtle pulling back, like the tide retreating. **The air grows lighter**, but your work is not yet finished. Walk with purpose, wayfarer, **counterclockwise**

around your circle. This path undoes what you have created, bringing closure to the sacred space. As you reach each candle, extinguish its flame one by one, and offer your thanks to the elements that stood sentinel.

"By black earth, by purple air, by brown waters, by red fire — I release the guardians of the circle. My work is done. Go in peace."

Each flame fades in turn, and with it, the guardians of the elements return to their distant realms. As the last candle's light dims into darkness, stand in the center of the now-closed circle. **Breathe deeply**. Feel the energy that once pulsed with intensity now settle into a calm, gentle hum. You have walked the shadowed path, faced the Dark Goddess, and now, you have returned to yourself. But you are changed.

Wayfarer, **you will never be the same.**

After the Ritual

The Dark Goddess is with you now, her essence woven into your being. **Her presence lingers quietly**, in the corners of your thoughts, in the space between breaths. She may not be seen, but you will feel her in the quiet moments of your day — in your dreams, in moments of stillness, and most profoundly, in the times of your greatest transformation. **Her lessons are rarely gentle**, but they are always true, always purposeful.

Be prepared, for her energy will challenge you, pushing you to confront the shadows you have long ignored. **The dark corners of your soul will no longer hide from her gaze**. Where you once saw fear, she will show you strength. Where you clung to old wounds, she will demand release. You called her forth, and now she walks with you.

Change will come. There is no escaping it, for the Dark Goddess does not enter your life without leaving her mark. You may find that old habits, beliefs, and relationships begin to shift, often in ways that are unexpected. **She brings the storm, but with it, the clarity that only comes after the rain.**

You will see her in the moments of quiet reflection, when the world around you stills and you are left with nothing but your thoughts. You will hear her voice in the whisper of the wind, **in the shadows cast by the moonlight**, and in the depths of your own intuition. She is the dark mirror of your soul, reflecting back what you need to see, not what you wish to see.

Wayfarer, do not fear her presence. You invited her into your life for a reason. **She is here to guide you**, to tear down what no longer serves you, and to help you rise from the ashes of your own transformation. Her power is fierce, but so is yours. You have the strength to walk this path, for the Dark Goddess would not have come to you if you were not ready.

Now, walk forward with the knowledge that you are not alone. **She is with you**, watching, guiding, and waiting for the next time you will call her forth. Until then, wayfarer, live with the understanding that the shadows are no longer something to be feared—they are the places where your power resides, waiting to be claimed.

You called her, and now she is with you.

If you need help during rituals

Wayfarer, if at any point during the ritual you feel the weight of the energies surrounding you becoming too intense, or if the presence of the Dark Goddess feels overwhelming, you may call upon **JHS GNS**—the forest spirit, both child and lover of the Goddess. His presence is a gentle yet powerful force, here to guide and protect you in the midst of your sacred work.

To summon him, close your eyes and begin to **visualize his form**—a faun, naked and unburdened, yet full of ancient strength. His legs are strong, rooted to the earth like the trees of the deepest woods, and his skin is pale and smooth, kissed by the light of dawn. His long, golden hair flows down his back like strands of sunlight, and his eyes—blue like clear, still water— hold the depth of forgotten mysteries. His face, androgynous and ageless, is neither fully masculine nor feminine, but a blend of both, radiating a serene and otherworldly beauty. Above his brow, antlers of a deer rise elegantly, twisting toward the sky, symbolizing his connection to the earth and the wilds.

He steps forward softly, emerging from the edges of your vision, from the spaces between worlds, where the forest and the shadows merge. You can feel his presence now—a calm, grounding force, balancing the intensity of the ritual. His energy is wild yet nurturing, a reminder that you are never alone in the darkness, for nature itself stands with you.

To call him forth, speak these words with intent:

"JHS GNS, spirit of the wilds, child-son and lover of the Dark Goddess, I summon you to guide me, to stand with me in this sacred space. By the stag's antlers and the soft earth beneath, come to me now and lend me your strength."

As you speak, **visualize him standing beside you**, his blue eyes meeting yours, offering silent reassurance. Feel the warmth of his presence as he steadies the energies around you, his role as both protector and guide clear. He is there not to interfere with your work, but to provide a safe passage through the shadows, a gentle force to balance the dark currents.

Should the energy of the ritual become overwhelming, **focus on his image**, on the strength of his legs, the calm in his eyes. He will help you navigate the intensity of the Dark Goddess's presence, guiding you safely through the ritual and ensuring that you remain grounded.

Once the ritual is complete, and you are ready to release him, thank him for his presence:

"JHS GNS, I thank you for your guidance and protection. Return now to the wilds, to the forests from which you came. I release you in peace."

As you speak these words, visualize him retreating back into the shadows, his form dissolving into the mist, until all that remains is the faint whisper of his presence—always there, ready to return when you call upon him again.

TABLE OF CORRESPONDENCES

Goddess	Herbs	Incense	Crystals	Plants
Hekate	Sage, Yew, Mandrake	Myrrh, Mugwort	Obsidian, Black Tourmaline	Cypress, Yew
Persephone	Mint, Pomegranate seeds, Parsley	Floral incense, Frankincense	Garnet, Ruby, Pomegranate	Wheat, Narcissus
Nyx	Lavender, Willow, Ivy	Resin, Black Sandalwood	Onyx, Black Obsidian, Jet	Nightshade, Poppy
Juno/Hera	Lotus, Lavender, Rose	Jasmine, Rose	Sapphire, Emerald	Pomegranate, Peony
Diana/Artemis	Mugwort, Cypress, Wormwood	Cedar, Pine	Moonstone, Amethyst, Silver	Oak, Cedar, Cypress
Medusa	Snake Root, Datura	Myrrh, Patchouli	Serpentine, Malachite, Black Onyx	Belladonna, Ivy
Sekhmet	Basil, Cinnamon, Catnip	Cinnamon, Amber	Carnelian, Tiger's Eye, Ruby	Sunflower, Red Poppy

Nephthys	Cypress, Poppy, Rosemary	Myrrh, Sandalwood	Obsidian, Hematite	Cypress, Blackthorn
Hathor	Rose, Chamomile, Jasmine	Frankincense, Rose	Malachite, Turquoise, Lapis Lazuli	Fig tree, Papyrus
Nut	Lotus, Jasmine, Myrrh	Frankincense, Sandalwood	Lapis Lazuli, Star Sapphire	Fig, Papyrus
Lilith	Patchouli, Wormwood, Mugwort	Dark Musk, Myrrh	Black Onyx, Garnet, Moonstone	Wormwood, Blackthorn
Inanna	Myrtle, Lilies, Rose	Frankincense, Rose	Garnet, Carnelian, Gold	Myrtle, Lilies
Ereshkigal	Cypress, Poppy, Dark Ivy	Frankincense, Dragon's Blood	Black Obsidian, Garnet	Dark Ivy, Cypress
Baba Yaga	Mugwort, Pine, Blackthorn	Pine, Mugwort	Black Tourmaline, Jet	Blackthorn, Oak
Marzanna	Belladonna, Vervain, Mugwort	Myrrh, Sage	Hematite, Black Onyx	Blackthorn, Belladonna

Kali	Hibiscus, Red Lotus, Wormwood	Jasmine, Sandalwood	Smoky Quartz, Red Tourmaline	Hibiscus, Lotus
Durga	Basil, Red Hibiscus, Bay	Sandalwood, Jasmine	Red Jasper, Carnelian, Ruby	Banana, Ashoka Tree
Chinnamasta	Mugwort, Hibiscus, Vervain	Sandalwood, Jasmine	Bloodstone, Obsidian	Hibiscus, Lotus
Chamunda	Mugwort, Bloodroot, Wormwood	Sandalwood, Blood Cedar	Obsidian, Smoky Quartz	Bloodroot, Datura
Hiḍimbā	Mugwort, Datura, Bloodroot	Myrrh, Dragon's Blood	Red Jasper, Obsidian	Datura, Acacia
Oya	Basil, Eucalyptus, Patchouli	Sandalwood, Cinnamon	Amethyst, Garnet, Red Jasper	Croton, African Violet
Yewa	Jasmine, White Lotus, Lilies	Jasmine, Rose	Rose Quartz, Amethyst, Pearl	Water Lily, Lotus
Morrigan	Belladonna, Vervain, Mugwort	Dragon's Blood, Sage	Black Obsidian, Garnet, Bloodstone	Blackthorn, Oak

Macha	Clover, Mint, Rowan	Frankincense, Cedar	Red Jasper, Bloodstone	Clover, Rowan
Badb	Mugwort, Vervain, Heather	Dragon's Blood, Myrrh	Obsidian, Hematite	Blackthorn, Hawthorn
Cailleach	Juniper, Heather, Ivy	Pine, Cedar	Smoky Quartz, Jet	Ivy, Yew
Hel	Henbane, Yew, Nightshade	Sandalwood, Cypress	Onyx, Black Tourmaline	Yew, Cypress
Skadi	Pine, Birch, Juniper	Pine, Cedar	Lapis Lazuli, Snowflake Obsidian	Birch, Pine
Angrboda	Hemlock, Wolfsbane, Mugwort	Myrrh, Mugwort	Black Onyx, Obsidian	Wolfsbane, Hemlock

CONCLUSION

Wayfarer, if you find yourself standing at the threshold of ancient mysteries, your curiosity is not misplaced. The allure of ancient cultures—woven with threads of mythology, magic, and forgotten rituals—has always beckoned those who seek something deeper, something beyond the veil of ordinary existence. It is the call of the past, of ancient deities whose power transcends time. But if you are here, perhaps it is not just history that intrigues you. Perhaps *she* is calling—the Dark Goddess herself, whispering through the winds of your life, summoning you to transformation.

The journey you've undertaken through these pages is not merely one of knowledge. It is an initiation. From the moment you opened this book, you began a path that few dare to tread— a path where shadows merge with light, and the divine feminine waits, veiled in darkness, to reveal her truth to you.

You did not come here to understand the deities of the past as distant figures locked in the pages of history. No, you came because *something within you* stirs. The Dark Goddess calls for those ready to embrace the profound and often unsettling truths that reside within. She transforms, not gently, but through fire and shadow, breaking down the old to reveal the raw, untamed power of the soul. And if she calls for you, know this: your life is about to shift in ways you may not yet comprehend.

You began by exploring the very essence of the Dark Goddess— her role as the embodiment of the shadow self, the unseen, and the unapologetic force of feminine power. Her energy is not soft;

it is primal. You felt her presence in the stories of Hecate, Persephone, and Nyx—Greek goddesses often misunderstood, whose dominion stretches from the underworld to the night sky, who are both feared and revered. These are not goddesses of peace but of power, transformation, and mystery.

Ancient Egypt, too, holds its share of dark and powerful figures. In Sekhmet, the warrior goddess, and Nephthys, guardian of the dead, you sensed the fierce protection of those who walk between worlds, where war and chaos coexist with medicine and healing. The Egyptian pantheon is steeped in the balance of life and death, and through these deities, the Dark Goddess manifests as both destroyer and nurturer.

From the sands of Egypt, you journeyed to the fertile crescent of Mesopotamia, where the goddess Ereshkigal reigns over the underworld. You tasted the bitterness of exile and sovereignty in her story—where death does not come as an enemy, but as a realm to be ruled. In Slavic mythology, you uncovered the chilling aspects of goddesses like Marzanna, who embodies winter's death, and the rebirth that follows. These figures, like the Dark Goddess herself, wield a power that is both terrifying and necessary.

And then there is Hindu culture, where the Dark Goddess takes many forms, from Kali's fierce dance of destruction to Chinnamasta's shocking sacrifice. These goddesses challenge your understanding of life and death, inviting you to see the divine even in chaos, even in endings. The Dark Goddess in Hindu mythology is a force of transformation, both feared and revered, as she tears down illusions and brings forth truth.

In Africa, you encountered the Orishas, goddesses like Oya who command the storms and walk with the dead. The spiritual energy of these deities, tied to nature and the elements, remind you that the Dark Goddess is not just a figure of the past. She is present, swirling through the winds and waters, grounding you in the earth beneath your feet. Her energy is raw and untamed, like the land itself.

Your journey continued through the mists of Celtic and Norse mythology, where the Dark Goddesses like the Morrigan and Hel reign over life, death, and everything in between. These are goddesses who do not shy away from the harsh realities of existence but embrace them fully. They ask you to confront the darkness within, to face the inevitable cycles of life, death, and rebirth, and to claim your power in doing so.

Wayfarer, you have not just read their stories—you have felt them, haven't you? These goddesses are not merely figures to be understood intellectually. They are energies to be embraced. They are calling for you to look deeper within, to connect with the shadow parts of yourself that you may have long ignored.

In learning about these deities, you have begun to awaken your own inner Dark Goddess. You have stepped into the transformative space where shadow meets light, where the feminine divine exists not in soft whispers, but in howling winds and roaring flames. The Dark Goddess is *within you*, waiting to be acknowledged, waiting for you to recognize her reflection in your own soul.

You've learned that embracing her requires a deep understanding of your own shadow self. You've delved into the psychological and spiritual aspects of this shadow work, learning how to integrate the hidden, often uncomfortable parts of yourself that you've repressed. The rituals and practices within these pages are not merely ancient relics; they are tools for your own spiritual evolution. They are offerings to the goddess within and guideposts for your own journey into the depths of self-discovery.

There is no going back now, Wayfarer. The Dark Goddess has seen you. She walks with you, in your dreams, in your quiet moments of contemplation, in the times when you feel your own strength surge through you. She is in the moments of transformation, when life seems to crumble around you, only to be rebuilt stronger and more aligned with your true self. Her lessons are not always easy, but they are always powerful.

You called her, and she has answered. Now, it is your turn to listen. Listen closely, for she will reveal to you the truths you need to hear. Her energy will challenge you, but it will also guide you toward a deeper understanding of who you are. This is the path of the Dark Goddess, and you, Wayfarer, are now walking it.

Be prepared, for she brings change. Be open, for she brings wisdom.

Claim Included Content

Congratulations on getting this book!
If you want to attract and manifest more Love and Abundance and Find Out about spirituality and topics, then join Templum Dianae's community and get guided meditation MP3 for awakening your inner self.

This guided meditation is designed to manifest your inner dream in your daily life.

templumdianae.com/en/bookmp3/

Bibliographical references
and recommended readings

- **Evolutionary Esoteric Numerology** - Templum Dianae Media - 2023
- **The Numbers of Angels** - Templum Dianae Media - 2023